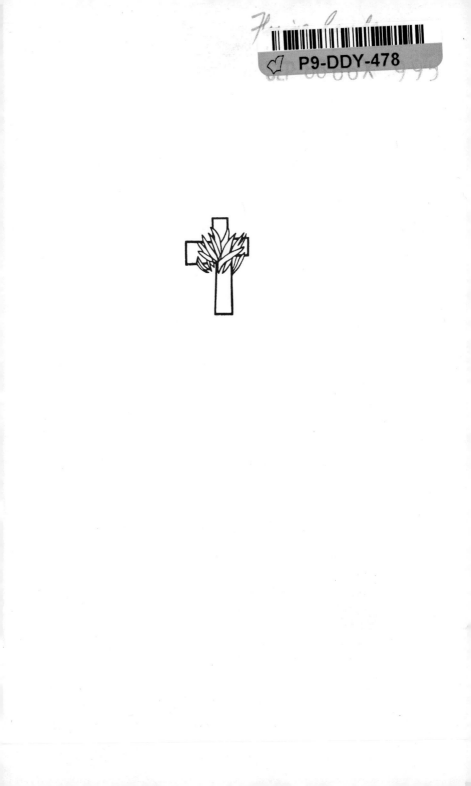

MESSAGE OF THE SACRAMENTS

Monika K. Hellwig, Editor

Christian Marriage

A Journey Together

by

David M. Thomas

Michael Glazier
Wilmington, Delaware

First published in 1983 by Michael Glazier, Inc., 1723 Delaware Avenue, Wilmington, Delaware 19806 and distributed outside the USA and Canada by Gill and Macmillan, Ltd., Goldenbridge, Inchicore, Dublin 8

Second printing with revised bibliography 1985.

Library of Congress Catalog Card Number: 82-84412
International Standard Book Number
  Message of the Sacraments series: 0-89453-280-4
  CHRISTIAN MARRIAGE:
    0-89453-231-6 (Michael Glazier, Inc.)
    7171-1137-7 (Gill and Macmillan, Ltd.)

Cover design by Lillian Brulc

Printed in the United States of America

Table of Contents

EDITOR'S PREFACE

This volume is one of the series of eight on *The Message of the Sacraments*. These volumes discuss the ritual practices and understanding and the individual sacraments of the Roman Catholic community. Each of the eight authors has set out to cover five aspects of the sacrament (or, in the first and last volumes, of the theme or issue under discussion). These are: first of all, the existential or experiential meaning of the sacrament in the context of secular human experience; what is known of the historical development of the sacrament; a theological exposition of the meaning, function and effect of the sacrament in the context of present official Catholic doctrinal positions; some pastoral reflections; and a projection of possible future developments in the practice and catechesis of the sacrament.

There is evident need of such a series of volumes to combine the established teaching and firm foundation in sacramental theology with the new situation of the post-Vatican II Church. Because the need is universal, this series is the joint effort of an international team of English-speaking authors. We have not invited any participants whose writing would need to be translated. While we hope that our series will be useful particularly to priests, permanent deacons, seminarians, and those professionally involved in sacramental and catechetical ministries, we also address ourselves confidently to the educated Catholic laity and to those outside the Roman Catholic communion who are interested in learning more about its life and thought. We have all tried to write so as to be easily understood by readers with little or no specialized preparation. We have all tried to deal with the tradition imaginatively but within the acceptable bounds of Catholic orthodoxy, in the firm conviction that that is the way in which we can be most helpful to our readers.

The Church seems to be poised today at a critical juncture in its history. Vatican II reopened long-standing questions about collegiality and participation in the life of the Church, including its sacramental actions, its doctrinal formulations and its government. The Council fostered a new critical awareness and raised hopes which the Church as a vast and complicated institution cannot satisfy without much confusion, conflict and delay. This makes ours a particularly trying and often frustrating time for those most seriously interested in the life of the Church and most deeply committed to it. It seems vitally important for constructive and authentically creative community participation in the shaping of the Church's future life, that a fuller understanding of the sacraments be widely disseminated in the Catholic community. We hope that many readers will begin with the volumes in this series and let themselves be guided into further reading with the bibliographies we offer at the ends of the chapters. We hope to communicate to our readers the sober optimism with which we have undertaken the study and thereby to contribute both to renewal and to reconciliation.

Monika K. Hellwig

INTRODUCTION

When authentic Christianity is translated into living form it becomes a love affair. At its widest and deepest point it involves God, absolute and eternal, loving and at least potentially being loved in return by every person born on the face of the earth. Yet to love God and no more is not enough because God desires a love that is thoroughly human, a love integrated with all that is part of human life. The first extension of the love of God is in the realm of human life which is the most personal, namely the sphere of the interpersonal. To paraphrase the demanding insight of John's first epistle, anyone claiming to love God without a corresponding love of neighbor is a liar.

As one scans the land in search of interpersonal love, a place where it can be found is in the very ordinary and common relationship of marriage. There, like a point where there can be found all the possibilities of intimacy in both a positive and negative form, the possibilities of intense Christian love are tested in a unique way.

As may be more apparent now than at any other period of Christian history, the successful accomplishment of this task is far from easy. Societal values based on a me-first philosophy accompanied by economic hardships brought on by massive changes in the final quarter of this century turn a lifelong and loving marriage into a precious and rare commodity.

For this reason it is appropriate and timely that the church do all within its power to support and assist the married in their attainment of marital success. Progams for marriage enrichment and pastoral assistance to those in need of counseling are being brought in the ordinary life of the church. Also helpful is the articulation of clear theologies of marriage which provide both direction and a sense that one is appreciated and understood in the effort to create a sound marriage. Struggle and strain without meaning is impossible to sustain. People give up when it is realized that one's effort has no real meaning or that nothing will come after the expenditure of energy. And sustaining a vital marriage certainly requires a major personal investment.

As some of the history of this theology is explored, it is apparent that a significant gap between the words of the theologians and the lives of married Christians was allowed to develop. Fortunately, this gap is now decreasing. Theologians are more concerned about the connection between the theories they spin and the practice it attempts to illumine and describe. The people of the church are more interested in pursuing the deeper meaning of their lives, and are becoming more conversant with the discussions of theology. Adult religious education in both formal and informal settings is spreading in local churches. As believers become more adult in their belief, they seek to learn not only what is to be accepted, but also the reasons behind formal principles. This is a healthy situation, but one which makes more demands of those entrusted with communicating the message of the Gospel, particularly the clergy and those professionals involved in the educational ministry of the church.

I note the importance of a joining of theologians with the people to situate my discussion of the theology of Christian marriage. It is my intent to formulate a theology of marriage both for those entrusted with the pastoral and educational care of the married, and for ordinary Christians seeking a deeper understanding of their marital life. Some historical and biographical background may be helpful in clarifying my concern. Whether theologians admit it or not, their trade is influenced by the "whens" and "whys" of their reflection and communication. The schools attended, the professors listened to, the books read, the conversations held, the meetings attended, all have their impact on the books and articles eventually published.

A significant experience for me took place in 1980 when I served as a *peritus* (advisor) to the United States bishop delegates who were participating in an international synod in Rome which had as its theme the Christian family. It was an exciting time as bishop representatives and a small contingent of lay people convened daily in the presence of John Paul II to discuss with candor and pastoral care the various gifts and needs of married and family Christians around the world. While the official purpose of the synod was to advise the pope, the gathering itself served as a sounding board for church thought on an international level. There surfaced a variety of personal viewpoints and theological opinions as delegates addressed the meeting from personal backgrounds and as representatives of Catholicism in a local area.

While no extended discussion of the formal theology of marriage occurred at the Synod of 1980, certain interventions (the official designation of positions formally entered into the synodal proceedings) stand out in my memory as both deeply insightful and promising of future developments in this area of theology. Most challenging was the intervention of Cardinal George Basil Hume of Westminster.

Based on his own theological and pastoral sensitivity, the Cardinal made the following intervention during the synod. "The prophetic mission of the family, and so of husbands and wives, is based upon their experience as married persons and on an understanding of the sacrament of marriage on which they can speak with their own authority. This experience and this understanding constitute, I would suggest, an authentic *fons theologiae* (source of theology) from which we, the pastors, and indeed the whole church, can draw."

It is in the spirit of this vision and in light of John Paul II's response to the Synod, his apostolic exhortation on the family, *Familiaris Consortio*, that I present my own contribution toward articulating an understanding of Christian marriage. While aware of the axiom common in the practice of psychological therapy that only a fool is his own or her own therapist, I cannot but help admitting to the influence of my own experience of marriage joined with countless conversations and observations of my contempories who also happen to be married. All through my formal theological education of more than twenty years (I still consider myself a learner), I have been particularly interested in what the formal theology of church had to say about this intriguing and challenging form of life. I became familiar with both the horror stories of the past, like the idea of St. Jerome that the best thing about marriage is that it produces virgins for the church, as well as excellent accounts of the nobility of life available to married Christians. I spent two years buried in the thought of Karl Barth, noted Protestant theologian, and his view of Christian marriage. My analysis of his approach became the substance of my doctoral dissertation at the University of Notre Dame.

In subsequent faculty appointments at Loyola University in New Orleans, St. Louis University in Missouri, St. Meinrad School of Theology in Indiana, and at Regis College in Denver, where I direct a graduate program in family ministry, I have researched and taught courses on marriage and family life. I also have benefited through my association with *Marriage and Family Living* magazine, a national publication which provided me with an opportunity to remain at the cutting edge of both Christian and secular wisdom as it continued to probe the deep, yet illusive truth of married life.

Over the years I have also profited by being a member of the United States Catholic Conference's National Commission on Marriage and Family Life. That commission was responsible in part for authoring a comprehensive vision and strategy of pastoral response to married and family Christians, and continues as a beacon of hope for those seeking success in these demanding areas of Christian life.

Perhaps more than any other area of theology, the theology of marriage is a theology of the people. Much of the interest in the theology of marriage comes from those formal movements or organizations in the church dedicated to strenghtening Christian marriage. I refer here to the growing number of persons associated with family ministry in the church, and to those movements which have been so instrumental in awakening for many a vision of that greatness to which married Christians are called.

It is fairly obvious that success in Christian marriage requires almost continual effort. Secular society cannot be interpreted as caring much about the survival of marriages despite widespread consensus that the health of society is traceable to the fundamental social units of marriage and the family. Timely then is the interest of all the major churches in supporting and enriching the marriages of their members. Today couples receive more preparation for marriage from the churches than ever before. There is also a rapidly growing number of programs for the already married. Both on the social and spiritual level (and these overlap in most instances) the churches are moving to involve couples as couples. It is worth recalling that it wasn't that long ago when men and women were separated in almost everything associated with formal church activity.

I have written this theology of marriage first for the married. My hope is that what I have written will encourage others to continue the search for understanding, as I have profited from those who have expressed their insights before me. I also write for those who as clergy or laity see their vocation as involving the care and support of married Christians.

I make no formal dedication of this book. My wife Karen would rather have me take out the garbage each night than find her name at the front of this book. Yet with the research and effort that goes into a project of this magnitude, I do have to acknowledge her patience and support along with that of our children who asked more than once when "it" would finally be finished. For them the book's completion

CHAPTER I:
"CHARTED IN THEOLOGY"

This book presents a theology of marriage. It is not intended as a manual for solving marital problems, or as a self-help guide on how to improve one's marriage. Rather, its basic goal is to bring forward into our time, with all its uniqueness and peculiarities, major insights of the Christian faith as they relate to married life. While respecting thoughtful formulation of the past, a living theology must be in the process of re-expressing itself as history unfolds. Ideally, the riches of theology are ever new, which, of course, reveals the precarious venture of theology. Protecting this uncertain effort is the fact that theology is as much the work of the individual theologian as it is the product of the community of theologians. Within the context of Roman Catholic theology, the theologian also operates within the framework of an ecclesial community entrusted by God with the conservation of the teaching of Jesus. Neither the theological nor the ecclesial community need be viewed as confining or restrictive. I would rather view both as directive, as summoning one ahead in creating new descriptions or fresh linguistic statements and arguments in support of the revelation of God's incredible love for humanity as evidenced most dramatically in the person of Jesus. This also means that the role of the theologians is as much one of being a listener and researcher as of being a thinker and communicator. I have sought to embody all these roles in formulating this account of the theology of marriage.

It is not debatable anymore that the institution of marriage is undergoing a major shift in emphasis in the Twentieth Century. Many books are published each year on marriage, sexuality, and family life, each attempting to provide, in its own way, answers to questions never before asked. Issues of intimacy, communication, lifestyle, childrearing, sexuality, fidelity, and so forth, while always part of married life, must now be discussed with nuances never before faced, even in the previous generation. The second Vatican Council was right on target in noting that, "Today, the human race is passing through a new stage of its history, . . . we can speak of a true social and cultural transformation, one which has repercussions on man's religious life as well."[1]

This transformation is acutely felt in the dynamics of human community. Perhaps the major question of our day concerns how we can live together. It is a question confronting nations; that is obvious. But it is also a question for the smallest human community: that of wife and husband. Profound human drama, with all the elements of the comic and the tragic, are played out daily in the fragile community of marriage. And while the human issues may be more apparent in marriage, beneath it all are important religious matters. In fact, right from the beginning of this book I want to state my contention that the human and the religious side of life can never be severed because all that is authentically human is rooted in the sacred: all creation is sacramental. And no place is this more important to reflect upon than in the consideration of interpersonal life in marriage.

---

[1]Vatican II, *Pastoral Constitution on the Church in the Modern World,* 4. (Throughout the book I will use the translation found in *The Documents of Vatican II,* edited by Walter M. Abbot, New York: Herder and Herder, Association Press, 1966.)

This book is about *Christian* marriage. It is written for today's followers of Jesus who want to blend their spiritual journey to God with the day-to-day events of married life. People came to Jesus, and now come to his church to be shown the "way." In the past, the church seemed more concerned about showing the way to the altar than the way to a better marriage. Today, however, there exists, in the church, a better appreciation of marriage as involving more than legalistic concerns. Pope John Paul II, in a recent document on marriage and the family, noted the importance of not only sound marriage preparation, but marriage enrichment as well.[2] This pastoral principle indicates a significant development in understanding Christian marriage as encompassing not only the wedding, but the totality of married life.

Since Christianity is more than pious phrases and noble sentiments, its formal language of theology must be translatable into the concrete substance of human life. While it would be most difficult, if not impossible, to create a theology of marriage which would be so specific and concrete that it would immediately apply to every marriage, it, nevertheless, is appropriate to demand a basic experiential aspect in theological discourse. Any theology, but particularly the theology of marriage, cannot be formulated as if no one ever lived its content, or could live its demands. In light of this principle, it is interesting to note the manner in which John Paul II formulates his understanding of Christian marriage. Right from the beginning of creation, he argues, marriage was designed to carry a profound message. In his own words, "the marriage of baptized persons thus becomes a real symbol of that new and eternal covenant sanctioned in the blood of Christ."[3]

What is the implication of this affirmation? Put into more down-to-earth language, it means that God's concern and

---

[2]Pope John Paul II, "The Apostolic Exhortation on the Family," *Origins* 11(1981), Section 56. (Subsequently this document will be referred to simply as "On the Family.")

[3]"On the Family," Section 13.

love for all people was to be embodied not only in word, but, more emphatically, in deed and in relationships. God designed certain created structures as capable of making present, in earthly guise, the very disposition or attitude which was made decisive and clear in the life and deeds of Jesus Christ. Christian marriage is also capable of playing a prominent role in being "a real symbol" of God's concrete love for humanity.

This divinely-intended meaning would not extinguish or deny the *human* meaning of the relationship. In fact, it would be *present in* the very substance of marriage itself. Any escape or disregard of the created human goodness of marriage would serve to block or vitiate God's sacred intent. Within the human dynamics of marriage, enriched and empowered by God, is what might appear as impossible to the skeptic or non-believer,that is, a genuine love. God's love is *real* and it can take on *human* form. And a privileged setting where that can and does happen is within the vital married life of Christians.

I believe that countless married Christians have lived, and live today quiet lives of great sanctity. Unfortunately, their stories rarely find a way into books or records listing the lives of the saints. In fact, there is no instance, to my knowledge, of a person being canonized simply because of being an exemplary spouse or parent. Priests, brothers, and sisters achieve saintly status by living outstanding Christian lives in accord with their particular vocation. The same criteria do not seem to apply in the case of married Christians, at least on the official ecclesiastical level.

Further, while most adult Christians are married and parents at significant stages of their lives, a historical survey of the literature of theology reveals little decribing the merits and virtues of the group which comprises the majority of church membership. With the exception of legal treatises on marriage, and often overly lengthy discussions concerning marital morality, there exists only what must be labeled scandalous silence about the importance of the role of married Christians to the life of the church. Solid and respected treatises on marital and family spirituality simply do not exist. One possible interpretation of this lack of published resources would be that married Christians were simply too busy *living* their faith and could not be bothered with getting the message in print.

An interesting exception to this silence exists in Christian history, but it has a strange twist. What might be called "the conjugal theme" is often used in the literature of spirituality. Yet in almost every instance, it does not refer to the sacred human love between wife and husband, but rather, to the individual soul's love affair with God. *The Canticle of Canticles,* now widely recognized as lyric poems sung during Hebrew wedding feasts, was interpreted in the church until recently as not referring to human love at all. Its literal meaning, and intent, that of being simply erotic poems spoken between the bride and groom, was dismissed as not being appropriate matter for an inspired book of the Bible. Both Origen (185-254), who penned a ten volume commentary on the *Canticle,* and Bernard of Clairvaux (1090-1153), who composed eighty-six sermons on the same book, treated the *Canticle* as simply an allegory of God's love. Both of these theologians had enormous influence within the church, particularly in formulating its spirituality. Some indication of Bernard's approach can be gained from the following passage: "Take heed that you bring chaste ears to this discourse of love; and when you think of these two lovers, remember always that not a man and a woman are to be thought of, but the Word of God and a soul."[4]

There can be no doubt that the church has consistently valued Christian marriage. But support often excluded an appreciation of the human, earthy, and sexual sides of marital life. Today, thanks largely to Vatican II the church no longer labors under this myopic theological position. Yet because this affirmation of Christian goodness in the *human* is only recent, it cannot be presumed *as present* unless clear evidence shows that this fundamental theological insight is operative.

---

[4]Bernard of Clairvaux, *Sermon on the Song of Songs,* 61.

Many people are surprised to learn that Matrimony was the last sacrament identified as belonging to the sacraments of the church. Their surprise stems in part, I believe, because so many adult Christians are married and almost instinctively experience their marriage as a major part of their Christian life. Yet, the fact remains that church theologians did not formally discuss the sacramental significance of marriage until the second millennium of Christianity.[5]

While history may reveal some hesitancy on the part of the church in identifying sacred qualities within marriage, present church teaching clearly takes an opposite view. Citing again the thought of John Paul II, he emphasizes that the essential message of God is expressed eloquently in Christian marriage:

> "The communion of love between God and people, a fundamental part of the Revelation and faith experience of Israel, finds a meaningful expression in the marriage covenant which is established between a man and a woman. For this reason, the central word of Revelation, 'God loves his people,' is likewise proclaimed through the living and concrete word whereby a man and a woman express their conjugal love."[6]

Nothing in church life today seems more critical or more important for the vitality of the total church than the living of the full Christian life within the interpersonal relationship of wife and husband. Christian marriage, when genuine, proves that deep and faithful love is really possible. No one, of course, would conclude that this type of love is easily realized. God's help is needed for empowering wife and husband to love each other in the unqualified manner implied in Christian marriage. Today it can be said that married life for Christians is not viewed as a peripheral matter in the church. Individual episcopal conferences are

---

[5]In chapter four a survey of the complex historical process through which Christian marriage was defined as sacramental will be presented.

[6]"On the Family," Section 12.

establishing marriage and family life as *major* pastoral *priorities*.[7] And it is not too soon for this to happen.

With societal pressures and philosophies often at odds with values consonant and supportive of marriage, it is both timely and helpful for Christians to possess a shared understanding of the unique *Christian* value of marriage. While it may seem like a private matter, marriage is either strengthened or weakened by the social setting in which it exists. The church community must supply what the secular community no longer offers: a vision of marital sanctity and the assistance needed to facilitate marital vitality. And this is, finally, being done. But most indicators show that the tasks are only in embryonic form. Church resources are scattered, and the vision is only beginning to gain proportion and structure.

It may be appropriate to mention here that it is healthy to be at least partially dissatisfied with every formal theological description of Christian marriage. While the imperfection of past theological descriptions is more easily explained, today's attempt to create a final description also merits censure. Humility is needed because the subject matter of this theological inquiry touches upon one of the most profound and mysterious elements in life itself: the meaning of love between persons.

Christians know that everything which passes between people also relates to their life with God. Whenever and wherever anyone affects or is affected by another, God, so to speak, gets into the act. The Christian life is essentially an interpersonal affair. And as this structural appreciation of the Christian life deepens, so will the theology of marriage improve.

As each aspect of Christian marriage comes up for consideration, it is the interpersonal dimension which invites reflection. If marital sex is discussed, it is the relational

[7]The foundational document for family ministry in the United States is *The Plan of Pastoral Action for Family Ministry: A Vision and Strategy,* Washington: United States Catholic Conference, 1978. A commentary on that document is to be found in David M. Thomas, *Family Life and the Church: A Manual for Leaders / Participants,* New York: Paulist Press, 1979.

aspect of sexuality which must be analysed. If fidelity is the issue, it is faithfulness between the spouses which is central.

Given the long-standing tradition in Western thought toward considering matters from the standpoint of the *individual* person, this relational side of life cannot be assumed. The Western bias for the rights, privileges, and autonomy of the private self compounds the difficulty in appreciating the role and value of interpersonal life. Often interpersonal life is appreciated only as instrumental or functional, as a process for fulfilling or completing the self. The motto "I need you to be me" illustrates this tendency. As long as interpersonal life is valued only as it serves the needs of private self, the profound significance of how love of God relates to love of neighbor will be missed. The neighbor will be valued only as a stepping-stone to God. As meaningful as this esteemed view of neighbor may appear on the surface, it falls far short of the view required for an adequate theology of interpersonal life, and its application to marital life. What a theology of Christian marriage most needs and deserves is an account which sets forth how the kind of human intentions, actions, and affections, sometimes thought to be reserved for God alone, can be directed toward one's marital partner. Without that kind of formulation, the demands of fidelity and exclusivity in Christian marriage will simply appear as idolatrous.

Vatican II broke new and decisive ground by describing Christian marriage as an "intimate partnership of married life and love."[8] The Council sought to emphasize the interpersonal dimension of marriage by linking it specifically to the divine covenant between God and the chosen people, between Christ and the church. Christian marital partnership creates a covenant between the wife and husband. The language of covenant was preferred to the more traditional, but too restrictive, language of contract. Yet, this newer formulation is only a first step in forming a more appropriate theology of Christian marriage for our time; it simply

[8]Vatican II, *Church in the Modern World,* 48. The original Latin is: *Intima communitas vitae et amoris coniugalis.*

creates a new framework which will guide future formulation. With full focus on the persons involved rather than rights or services exchanged, and with stress on the totality of the relationship rather than on specific acts, the theology of marriage will become more expansive in nature. Loss of the type of precision required by a legalistic approach will occur because greater respect will be shown to the personal characteristics of the marital union.

An adequate theology of marriage will also take into account that each concrete realization of Christian marriage will be unique. The "matter" for the Sacrament of Matrimony is a particular woman and a unique man. Thus a theological description of Christian marriage will include space for filling in the names of both the wife and the husband. In an important sense, therefore, no two sacramental manifestations of marriage can be identical. There may be similar intentions and lifestyles present in many marriages, but each will also express unique characteristics and patterns. Each Christian marriage will be a "once-and-for-all-time" sacramental event displaying different aspects of God's covenantal love within the relational life of the couple. This principle, once again, may possibly cause headaches for the legalistic mind which seeks common factors shared by all cases. Yet, as I see it, the inclusion of "a principle of particularity" in the theology of marriage is necessary to respect the reality it is intended to describe.

Having said that, I would not like to leave the impression that each Christian marriage results in being whatever one wants. Unallayed relativism is as fallacious as absolutism. Following the Lord has specificity in determining a general orientation to life and thought. Yet, the personal embodiment of that orientation requires a translation into each concrete marriage relationship.

The blending of the objective with the subjective, the abstract with the personal, has always been a challenge for theology. It is, therefore, useful to understand something about theological method because the manner in which the subjective and objective is resolved will strongly influence the shape of a theology of marriage.

Christian theology is ultimately based on experiences of God. Some of this experience can be found scattered throughout the Bible, and is, at times, "first hand" reporting. Yet, most of what we find there, even in the gospels, is "second hand" narration.

Once removed from the experience, narrations tend to become more abstract, although this need not be judged as a liability. A more generalized account can allow many people to see themselves related to the event. This is what occurred in the early church for those who were not eyewitnesses to the events of the life of Jesus. In hearing and reading about the events, they saw new possibilities, new ways of thinking and acting in their own lives. They saw themselves in a new light. Their imaginations were inspired to conceive of new ways of living. In this way the so-called objective or abstract decription served the subjective as a kind of framework for understanding, as an indicator to a new path of action.

A helpful image for appreciating the role of theology in one's personal life was suggested forty years ago by C. S. Lewis. He noted that theology's functional value could be appreciated more fully if it were thought of as a map. Maps provide two important benefits. First, maps are constructed from countless observations of those who sailed the full expanse of all the oceans, who traveled throughout the lands. Maps *put into perspective* single observations of anyone anywhere in the world. Second, maps are useful when one begins a journey into areas where one has no experience. Maps in that case *set direction* toward a desired destination. Good theology should function like maps drawn from the experiences and interpretations of many travelers along God's way. They can warn us of pious excesses (which may or may not be genuine experiences of God), or they can suggest a direction most likely to bring us into real contact with the Lord.

The basic image used in this book is that of a shared journey. Wife and husband blend each one's personal odyssey into a common passage to God. It is best to imagine them as side-by-side, rather than one as leader with the other as follower. Their map-reading activity respects the ability of both to decipher which way is best for them together. Each one's pace is personal, as is what each acquires along the way. Their bond is one of love, not of mechanical bonding. How well they progress along the way will depend partly on how well they relate to each other. Each will bring maps already used up to the time of their marriage. And one of the first tasks confronting them will be the sharing of personal maps. Then will begin the constructing of a new map based on each one's "old" maps along with research in maps of the church and those drawn by other married Christians. The new map will chart the first steps in their journey together.

Theology can then be thought of as having a very practical purpose. It should use language accessible to all who might profit from its descriptions. Unwillingness to avail oneself of the insights and directives of good theology raises the chances that one will embark on an errant life journey. One might create all kinds of out-dated, silly, even harmful ideas about God and the human situation. Theologians are not infallible; but when they responsibly exercise their craft, what results is worth a hearing, particularly in areas touching everyday life.

To be personal, I have found the map image very useful in conceiving of the theologian's role. As I formulate a theology of marriage, my goal is to point out promising directions, as well as dangerous extremes. My intent is to underline and decribe the roads travelled by ordinary married Christians. While not wanting to skirt important theological debates (about this road or that), I want to concentrate more on those features of the map which pertain to the journey where there is substantial agreement among the map-makers. My hope is that what follows will provide a helpful theological wisdom for the ordinary, day-to-day events of the marriage.

A contemporary theology of sacramental marriage, therefore, passes through some rather familiar territory. It discusses the mystery of sexuality, the dynamics of marital love, the stages of conjugal growth, the responsibility of creating new life, and the demands of fidelity and exclusivity. While respecting traditional insight, good theology cannot be content to simply restate past formulations, however excellent they may have been. It is challenged to restate in the context of its own setting, sensitive descriptions born of new resources, and those particular winds of the Spirit each age experiences. As more travellers make the journey, maps may require redrawing. The maps have to fit the facts. New emphasis may be needed to express the kind of special Christian witness appropriate to today's Christian marriages.

For example, the more traditional theological focus on the procreational dimension of Christian marriage is now being complemented by a theology which emphasizes the love relationship between the wife and husband. This does not imply the total replacement of one focus by the other, but a clear shift toward a greater value accorded the conjugal relationship. Earlier maps were drawn when the population was low. This is no longer the case. What appears needed today is greater emphasis on marital love, which seems, to many, to be in short supply. Likewise, the meaning of fidelity and exclusivity merit reconsideration as qualities meaningful to today's Christian couples. The times have called forth this emphasis on loving fidelity. The value of lifelong marital love is under attack. Christian realism responds accordingly. Also, general developments in biblical scholarship and historical theology point out the centrality of love in mapping Christian existence. This is not a compromise of values at all. Rather, the relational emphasis flows from responsibly reading the signs of the times, and discerning the appropriate Christian response. The maps must be redrawn.

Cooperating with God in the salvation of the world may seem on the surface to be a rather abstract task. Yet, when the concept is converted into action, based on the dynamics of human life today that are harmonious with God's intent for creation, it becomes concrete and vital. For something to be "saved" means that it is moved in the direction pointed out by God's plan, which is not an abstract blueprint, but an ongoing love affair between God and creation.[9]

When Jesus was asked about marriage, he referred his listeners to God's original intent in creating humans as female and male. He reminded them of Genesis. He invited them to rethink some of the information they already knew. The role of the Christian community today is the same. Its continuous role is to unpack the connection between God's intent for humanity and specific issues, for example, the survival of marriage. This is primarily a theological task which looks first to God's revelation as received and understood by the church, and joins that analysis with human existence challenged by the exigencies of the present. Part of that reflective process should also be related to that knowledge and experience of God, and God's intent, gained by married Christians as they live out their marital commitments. "Ivory tower" or theoretical thinking is most inappropriate in theological reflections on Christian marriage.

More than anything else the *religious* meaning of marriage is sought. It is drawn from life itself, particularly by those guided by God's Spirit in the church. The inquiry should include the conversations of married Christians. It is even related to the private dialogue between wife and husband. The pursuit of truth and meaning is unending, as are all attempts to define the Mystery in which human life is set. But genuine progress is possible for both the individual and the community if the evidence surfaced within the Christian experience of marriage is honestly evaluated, if the procedures of logic are followed, and if the community remains sensitive to the key elements of revelation particularly as spoken and lived by Jesus. A creative tension between the old and the new is inevitable. A special kind of courage will be needed to accept new insights or new paths which may not appear evident on maps drawn for other periods of history.

[9]See Rosemary Haughton, *The Passionate God,* New York: Paulist Press, 1981, p. 90.

As was already noted, Vatican II began its description of Christian marriage by "mapping" it as an intimate partnership of life and love. It is, therefore, with that emphasis on Christian conjugal love that the theology of marriage offered here begins. With all life rooted in God's love and with that same pattern operative in Christian marriage, all formal theological discussion of marriage must begin with an analysis of Christian marital love. Good theology has the ability to draw God more "out into the open." While God is believed to be present everywhere, as will be the testimony of any youngster in catechism class, God is not there in any obvious way. This is partly what is meant by naming God as Mystery. With the New Testament defining God finally as love itself, we are alerted to seeking God, particularly in the experience of married love.

The history of the theology of Christian Marriage exhibits a pattern in which the content of the sacrament becomes more and more refined. The church was interested in defining those features whose presence indicated that the sacrament was authentically present. Its concern was largely legalistic as it needed precise categories for determining sacramentality, or more practically, the absence of a sacramental dimension in a given marriage, its juridical interest can be understood and appreciated.

In the theological analysis of marriage expressed in the chapters to follow, I will move in somewhat of a different direction. Rather than searching out a minimalistic description of the sacrament, I want to mine all the riches of matrimony exposing its meaning in accord with the many facets of married life. I see Christian marriage as a prism through which shines God's love into many areas of human life. Exploring their meaning forms the outline of the following chapters. Through the love of wife and husband, woman and man, through loving words pronounced in public in formal ceremony and unfolded in the time that ensues through the couple's collaboration with God's creative power in bringing new life into the world, through the spirituality lived in transforming creation, sacrament of marriage brings the Spirit of God into the world. Each couple has the power to block this process, but what is more important to affirm is their capacity to advance it. And it happens. With that hopeful note we begin.

CHAPTER II:
FOUNDED ON LOVE

Jesus was a great teacher. He had a remarkable ability to take the ordinary folk wisdom of his day and apply it in illustrating the various aspects of life in the Kingdom of God. For instance, in laying the foundation for the kingdom, he said that if it was intended to stand for a long time, it should be built on rock, not on sand. Edifices found on moving sand would eventually sag and crumble. The wise builder, therefore, first inspects the ground well before the foundation is laid. Care taken in the beginning will prevent problems later on. This is good advice for all builders.

A theology of marriage for today must be founded on love. There is no other option. But the foundation of love has many of the characteristics of sand. Love is partly emotional, and subject to all kinds of ups and downs. The concept of love has even been taken from the sacred space between lovers and used to sell everything from soft drinks to sports cars. And when thought to be part of concrete relationships, it is customary to identify almost any level of attraction as love. People claim that they love people whom they hardly know. Love, as it is used today, appears as one of the "sandiest" words in the language.

Yet despite this, Christian marital love will be the foundation upon which all that follows in this book will be established. To insure that the concept of love used here is understood correctly, this chapter will attempt to identify its key characteristics. Unfortunately, no other word describes that which is central to the Christian vision or way of life.

Love is the most treasured, non-negotiable feature of the Christian life. This is founded on the fact that we are all first called into existence by God's love. Our response to God's love, according to Jesus, is expressed primarily in loving our neighbor. Yet because our understanding of religion is so deeply influenced by the cultural values of our time, the definition of Christian neighbor may be vague or illusive. As already noted, our society is inconclusive about love. The issue is further muddled by the way love of neighbor is discussed in a Christian context. The discussion often creates images of sentimental love, a love that is purely spiritual, or a love which represses certain areas of human life, particularly those relating to the sexual.[1] When applied to marriage, Christian principles are felt by some to restrain or curb the erotic, which at the same time also puts the marriage partners in some sort of straightjacket in order to maintain marital permanence and fidelity.

No longer, of course, is this approach found in the major documents of the church, or in the writings of contemporary theologians. In the books, at least, there is a widespread appreciation for the value and beauty of creation as fashioned by God. Sin has entered the world, but it has not brought about "total corruption." The world and human nature are still sound, in need certainly of divine assistance, but that help is more in terms of support, than of restriction. Today, the task before us is to create a positive set of statements, reinforcing the claim that God's loving plan for the married is in the very best interests of Christians who are seeking a blend of Christian and marital existence. A basic goal of this book is to contribute to the ongoing conversation which searches for a deeper vision and seeks to establish

[1]Daniel Day Williams, *The Spirit and Forms of Love,* New York: Harper and Row, 1968, p. 13.

connections between marital life and all the major elements of the Christian life.

Love of Neighbor as Person

While it might be assumed that marital love is always an interpersonal phenomenon, nevertheless, I feel it is beneficial to make the point quite explicit. My justification for perhaps belaboring the obvious is based on speculation that people can be involved more with the *idea* of love than with loving real people. And I would add that "religious" people seem particularly prone to this misplaced emphasis.

Fortunately, most contemporary treatises on Christian love emphasize strongly the concrete aspect of that love.[2] Other significant virtues are often interrelated with love, too, such as justice and obedience. This insures a practical and realistic dimension to love. When Jesus, the Man for others, is described, his specific acts of love and kindness are underlined.

To emphasize love's interpersonal meaning, one should first call to mind the way the self consciously and consistently is concerned about the happiness and enrichment of the beloved. To personalize this: I love another, a person whom I value, and I seek through my own resources, whatever they might be, to assist the person I love in his or her own betterment. If my love is genuine, it will be related to the concrete, the practical, and the explicit. It will be based on a responsible judgment of all that is most beneficial for the beloved. In the process of loving, I will necessarily extend myself in interest and concern beyond my own personal need toward assisting the beloved in meeting her or his needs. Thomas Aquinas believed that the essence of this

[2]Recommended books on this are: Robert Johann, *The Meaning of Love,* New York: Paulist, 1966; Morton Kelsey, *Caring: How Can We Love One Another?,* New York: Paulist, 1981; Gene Outka, *Agape: An Ethical Analysis,* New Haven: Yale University Press, 1972; Joseph Pieper, *About Love,* Chicago: Franciscan Herald Press, 1974 and George Tavard, *A Way of Love,* Maryknoll: Orbis Books, 1977.

orientation was the desire on the part of the lover that the beloved live and live well.[3]

Philosophically, this attitude of personal love can be called its self-transcending quality. Given is the belief that we all tend to think of ourselves first, that we prioritize as highest our own personal needs, whether they be corporeal, psychological, or spiritual, before those of anyone else. When we truly love another, this whole process of me-first is changed as the needs of another person are allowed to influence personal choice. Someone else counts in personal reckoning. In the personal decision-making process, where interest, time and resources are allocated, I include my beloved in my calculations. Using the language of resource-management brings home the point quite graphically because it is contemporary, and it surfaces more clearly how loving another person actually changes the way one thinks and lives. Personal love is practical love. It possesses emotional qualities, but if truly authentic, it will also affect the fundamental orientation of virtually all personal decisions. Joined together is the desire to be with the other, and the decision to act for the other.[4] Mere sentiment is translated into action which, in turn, serves as an enriching nutrient for personal growth. The act of genuine love becomes, in fact, the central act of personal development, particularly as it forms a basis for decisions and actions in daily life.[5]

Also beneficial for understanding Christian love is to grasp how the concrete love of neighbor is integrally bound up with one's love of God. For, without this insight, the kind of demands and commitment required by Christian neighborly love in general, and marital love in particular, would seem almost idolatrous. Also, unless this point is clarified many passages in the New Testament will appear as utter nonsense. Clear thinking here will also help married Christians realize that the total love offered to the marriage

[3]Thomas Aquinas, *Summa Theologiae,* II, II, 25, 7.

[4]An excellent analysis of this is found in Rollo May, *Love and Will,* New York: W. W. Norton and Co., 1969.

[5]Karol Wojtyla (Pope John Paul II), *The Acting Person,* Boston: D. Reidel Publishing Co., 1979.

partner is not, in fact, a compromise of their love of God.

In Matthew's Gospel, for example, Jesus addresses Peter with the following statement: "Moreover, everyone who has given up home, brothers and sisters, father and mother, wife and children or property for my sake will receive many times as much and inherit everlasting life" (Mt. 19:29).

How is the married Christian to interpret these words to Peter? My own reaction, as a husband/father, is that I cannot imagine any circumstances under which it would be right to sever these relationships, even for the sake of Jesus. Much of my personal religious faith centers around the belief that it is God's will that I continually seek to deepen, not weaken, and certainly not sever the bonds of love which tie me to my wife and children. Could it be possible that Jesus is suggesting an incompatibility between full discipleship and a whole-hearted commitment to spouse and children? Or is there still room for both forms of adherence, joining full commitment to marriage and family with full discipleship of the Lord?

A reading of Jesus' words in Matthew's gospel must take into account the specific setting of the passage. From time to time the disciples wondered whether their leaving of home, possessions, and, even family, was really worth the cost. In this specific section of Matthew's gospel, we find the familiar story of the rich young man who declined the invitation of discipleship because of his many worldly attachments. It is important, therefore, to notice how Matthew combines a discussion of possessions with that of family. The intent of Jesus here seems more related to the incompatibility of security based on possessions (both goods and family) with the risk needed for full participation in the Kingdom of God.

The point, therefore, is not a rejection of marriage and family life in itself, but a specific meaning attached to family life in Jesus' time: its ability to seemingly provide all that is needed in life. Jesus responds that there is more to life than security based on possessions and family membership. These cannot deliver the rewards of eternal life. He was also reminding Peter quite simply that he made a good choice.

The rewards will eventually outweigh the costs. If the whole context of the passage is taken into account, Jesus is not even dealing with the issue of married life versus discipleship. In fact, he never does. Here he commends Peter, implicitly at least, for his generous response to the Lord's call, but does not offer a universal principle that regards marriage and family life as opposed to discipleship.[6]

There exists no incongruency because of the relationship between the two great Commandments: love of God and love of neighbor. One of the best analyses of this point was done by Karl Rahner, the respected German theologian.[7] Without going into the rich intricacies of his thought, I will simply offer a summary of his argument.

First, he correctly affirms that the only relationship worthy of full human commitment is relationship to God. But he also notes that this divine relationship stands more as a background or horizon for the enactment of our concrete expressions of love, which is the way we, as concrete persons, must express ourselves. In some measure our love for God can only be expressed in a manner related to our status as being in the world. While the source and power for establishing these relationships come from God, our loving orientation and activity properly focuses on concrete objects or persons. This is necessary for our Christian love to be truly human and to flow from our identity as being created in this world. Rahner concludes his reflection by stating that the love of neighbor is the only type of human act capable of embodying full commitment to God. Supporting his argument are the words of the first letter of John: "If anyone says, 'My love is fixed on God,' yet hates his brother, he is a liar. One who has no love for the brother he has seen cannot love the God he has not seen" (1 John 4:20).

In Rahner's view, therefore, only the concrete neighbor is a proper focus for Christian love. The neighbor is not in

[6]See John P. Meier, *Matthew* (New Testament Message Vol. 3), Wilmington: Michael Glazier, 1980, pp. 218-226.

[7]Karl Rahner, "Reflections on the Unity of the Love of Neighbor and the Love of God," *Theological Investigations* VI, New York: Seabury, 1974, pp. 231-249.

competition with God as a proper object of Christian love; rather, neighbor love becomes the concrete way love for God is expressed. This conclusion rings true for all, but it has special implications for married Christians.

In Christian marriage love for God is meshed with love for one's spouse. The link between loving God with one's whole heart and doing the same with one's spouse is allowed to develop without worry that God is being short-changed. Unless a harmony between the two loves is accepted and appreciated, the substance of what follows may well appear as a puzzle with too many missing pieces.

Responsibility as Part of Authentic Love

In popular song and verse, love is often described as an expression of fate, a force lying outside human control or design. It befalls the lucky, and escapes the hapless. Unpredictable is the destination of Cupid's arrow.

The belief that there is something about love which is outside human control is not totally unfounded. Interpersonal mutual attraction is not something that can be simply willed into existence. In the context of marriage, while the premise that "there is only one in the world for me," is clearly debatable, initial meeting of one's eventual spouse may contain elements of chance or good fortune. People do stumble upon one another. Therefore, as is often noted in considering the initial stages of a relationship, fate, chance or luck can play an apparent role in establishing a given relationship.

Yet if a love relationship is to develop, more and more will depend on each person taking personal responsibility for the continuance of the relationship. Some discussion of responsibility is an essential part of Christian neighbor love, especially in its exemplification in marital love.

It is also timely to reflect on the role of responsibility in marital love because society today seems to offer little or no support for the survival of particular marriages. In the past, particularly in social groups which maintained an extended family system, intact marriage was valued. While it may not have been a result of conscious planning, the best interests of society were served by maintaining stable, solid, social relationships throughout the community. And as far as we can determine, this was accomplished with relative effectiveness. The conclusion here is not that marriages in the past were superior to those of today, but only to note that the social setting for marriage today has changed by becoming less supportive. Therefore, if a given marriage is to survive it will have to depend more on its own internal resources and strengths.[8]

Good theology can be of genuine assistance for Christians who are married by providing them with insight into how Christian marriage plays a central role in the general drama of Christian life. It can also direct their religious motivation and convictions toward doing all that is within their power to deepen their marital love. Also, a church alerted to the role of marriage in its own life can marshall its pastoral resources more effectively in support of marital vitality.[9]

Before Karol Wojtyla was elected pope, he wrote extensively about the need for responsibility in nurturing marital love.[10] We find the same theme developed in the writings of the esteemed Protestant theologian, Karl Barth. For him, Christian marriage is essentially a task to accomplish; it is like a work of art jointly fashioned by the mutual effort of wife and husband.[11]

Ethical responsibility, therefore, surfaces in Christian marriage as an element within marital love. It prompts the couple to "work" on their marriage. They ought not take each other for granted, nor can they assume that their love

---

[8]See David and Vera Mace, *How to Have a Happy Marriage,* Nashville: Abingdon, 1977 and Herbert Otto (editor), *Marriage and Family Enrichment: New Perspectives and Programs,* Nashville: Abingdon, 1976.

[9]This is a major theme in John Paul II, "On the Family."

[10]Karol Wojtyla, *Fruitful and Responsible Love,* New York: Seabury, 1979, pp. 18-19 and also his *Love and Responsibility,* New York: Farrar, Straus and Giroux, 1981, pp. 130-135.

[11]Karl Barth, *Church Dogmatics,* III/4, Edinburgh: T. and T. Clark, 1961, pp. 187-189.

will remain vital without effort. This task is part of their Christian discipleship, their vocation of expressing within their relationship the active love of God working to transform the world in a kingdom of love.

Christian marital love, because it is designed by God to carry such significance, will have certain qualities not readily apparent in a purely secular framework of understanding. Its definition will be primarily grounded in theology, not in humanistic thought. Yet the Christian love between wife and husband will be thoroughly human. Such humanness need not be thought of as foreign to a deeper meaning which includes God's creative and redemptive love. Attention is now focused on some of the special characteristics of this love made rich and fruitful by the power of the Lord.

The Shape of Marital Love

Christian marital love is a special type of neighbor love. In terms of depth and duration it is singular among human relationships. In sharing their journey, wife and husband walk life's path together, each supporting the other wherever the path leads. In freedom, they choose one another as the primary exemplification of neighbor love. There will be times, of course, when attention must turn to others, for instance, when their children or the needs of those outside the family demand consideration. But these "outside interests" are best seen as extensions or as an overflow of marital love. The love between wife and husband, just like God's love, creates new reality outside itself. The teaching of Vatican II emphasizes the prior status of the marital relationship while noting at the same time its creative potential for enrichment outside itself.[12] Christian marriage is not designed by God to isolate the couple from the outside world. Rather, it puts them at the very heart of the world from which life is generated. Like the sun, Christian marital

---

[12]Vatican II, *Church in the Modern World,* 50 and 51. This will be discussed at length in chapters six and seven.

love creates energy needed for life to survive across the face of the earth.

This same foundational quality of marriage is found in the Genesis accounts of creation. The passage is well-known, coming immediately after the Elohist story of the creation of woman out of the man's rib. If you take into account the cultural setting when it was originally composed, it carries a somewhat surprising message: it affirms that the marital relationship takes precedence over the relationship to one's family of origin. Almost offhandedly the author of the passage notes: "That is why a man leaves his father and mother and clings to his wife, and the two of them become one body" (Gen. 2:24).[13]

It is as if to say that no person in her or his right mind would dispute that the marital relationship is the most important relationship for humankind. The creation of a kind of self-standing marital community is established by leaving one's family of origin. Marriage arises, so to speak, from the ashes of one's original family.

In today's world this process of separation may seem to be something quite ordinary or natural. Yet, in a culture which valued highly the clan or extended family, as did the culture of early Judaism, the concept of leaving home and family to establish a marriage was indeed remarkable.

We can only speculate as to why the separation was called for. Even modern marriages often have difficulties in "cutting the cord" from parents and/or in-laws. On a practical level, whether it's best for those newly married or for their parents is not clear; there are probably benefits and losses for both. What seems most central, however, is the way relational priorities are established: disengagement precedes engagement; the marital relationship was to be constituted before all else. The most "competitive" relationship for marriage when the Genesis text was penned was that of one's family of origin. Genesis concludes that it should be

---

[13]The New American Bible supplies the following clarification with its translation: "One body: literally 'one flesh'; classical Hebrew has no specific word for 'body.' The sacred writer stresses the fact that conjugal union is willed by God."

put in second place. To apply this lesson today may signify the necessity to separate not only from family, but also from the "single lifestyle" or from old friends who cannot accept someone who chooses a marriage partner before them. Also competing with marriage might be a career which seeks to take one's full attention. The mandate of the Genesis text may have as much, if not more meaning, today than when it was first written.

Another interesting feature in the passage is its approach to the procreative meaning of marriage. While the value of securing off-spring is a central part of the overall approach to marriage in Scripture, this fact is not even mentioned in this passage. Silence concerning this point is significant. The passage leaves us only with an image of a solitary couple, pulling away from parental bonds so that they can stand together as a new community before the Lord. The simplicity of this portrait is suggestive of a meaning not at all obvious from a worldly standpoint.

Another significant feature in the establishment of marriage is its basis in freedom. While not evident in the Genesis text, as the meaning of Christian marriage developed, it became clear that the decision to marry must be done in freedom, without force or fear, either physical or psychological.[14] Marriage based on love requires a specific decision informed by knowledge and founded in freedom to join one's life with another for a lifelong journey. This decision cannot be any less than a thoroughly human act, responsive to oneself and to the person one is marrying, and finally to God before whom the marriage will be enacted, when the two become one flesh.

Reflections on the Concept: Two In One Flesh

Marital life, structured according to the Genesis mandate, will involve a process which results in transforming the

[14]Preparation for marriage will be discussed in chapter four.

two, wife and husband, into one flesh. No other biblical image is more closely associated with Christian marriage. The common interpretation given this text in the past was that it referred to the sexual union of the couple. Yet in light of today's understanding of marriage, the image ought to apply to more than biological mating. It refers specifically to the love relationship established in marriage. But even that general restatement needs clarification.

First, it is important to note that Christian marriage is not designed to deny or blot out the unique individuality or personality of either partner for the sake of some blended identity. Marriage is not a fusion of two individuals; rather, it involves the encounter through which they join their lives into a common project of sharing their journey toward God.

The joining of wife and husband ought to create a fuller life, a more complete existence for each. For this to happen both partners must love with a love that is seasoned and mature. A useful distinction in this context points to the difference between "gift-love" and "need-love." While all human love is probably a mixture of both, the emphasis in Christian marital love falls on gift-love, an offering of one's talents, insights and deeds to one's spouse. There is genuine giving, but also receiving, exchange, and sharing. And as their love deepens, there is less and less calculation relating to who is giving or receiving because their interchange is rooted in freedom. While not taking each other for granted, their sharing is more spontaneous.

This mutuality of sharing interests, concerns, and activities need not result in a depletion of either spouse. In fact, their sharing can be creative and enriching for both, augmenting everything each brings to the marital relationship. As each partner extends toward the other, there can be mutual enrichment on all levels of life. Teilhard de Chardin captured this point well. He wrote, "In every practical sphere, true union does not confound, it differentiates."[15] In

---

[15]Teilhard de Chardin, "The Grand Option," in *The Future of Man,* New York: Harper and Row, 1966 and Eric Fromm, *The Art of Loving,* New York: Harper and Row, 1956.

the sphere of interpersonal love, he noted that the only energy in the world which does not destroy the individual upon being united with another reality, is the energy of love. Love is creative, not destructive. It brings out what is best in each individual.

Marriage seen in this light is quite dynamic, constantly expanding in proportion to the couple's interpersonal generosity and openness. Should opposite tendencies prevail, the marriage will suffer diminishment.

Up to this point most of what has been described as Christian marital love focused on the positive. I wanted some of the "good news" about marriage announced before the all-too-comon horror stories were told. My reason for starting with positive, or the ideal, was to erect the description of Christian marriage on a foundation dependent on the power of the Risen Christ to bring to fruition, with human cooperation, the intent of God for marriage expressed "in the beginning." God's demands are not unrealistic, nor is God's help insufficient for achieving success. Inadequacy is always from the human side, either based on personal weakness or societal insufficiency.

Sin and selfishness are part of everyday affairs. As much as anything else, this surely impacts on marriage where the attempt to form a love-community is so vulnerable to human imperfection. Christian marriage is an ideal. A full realization of its potential probably borders on the heroic. But Christ never sought to compromise the ideal because, for him, the ideal was possible in the setting of God's kingdom. He also clearly knew the human condition and made extraordinary provision for those who might fail so that they could be reinstated as active contributors to the building of the kingdom.

Christian marriage is always open to and in need of further growth. Like the general life of the church, it never outgrows its pilgrim status. Its life is parallel to that of the spiritual life; all are, so to speak, "on the way" to perfection. And it is always helpful to have some sense of the destination. This is part of the purpose for sketching Christian marital love in what may seem to be quite idealistic categories.

An example of this idealism is found in recent church documents where Christian marriage is described in the language of "mutual self-bestowal,"[16] or "the love by which a man and a woman commit themselves totally to one another until death."[17] The giving of the self to another should not be interpreted as a type of donation which leaves the giver empty or depleted. Marital love as self-gift can be misunderstood, particularly if it is related to an out-dated understanding of sacrifice.

Christianity is solidly based on a positive value supporting life. It is also built on the hope that God's good creation will come to its intended destiny. While sacrifice is central to the Christian life, it is related more to the intention of "making holy" than the pagan notion of destroying a victim for God. Jesus came to serve humanity and expressed throughout his life, even to its last moment in death on the cross, the extent of his love. The cross must be understood in relationship to the life which preceded it, especially the interpretation Jesus gave to his life at the Last Supper when he washed His disciples' feet. This giving of his life for others did not result in him becoming less a human being, but rather, it exemplified how all are to live if they are to live abundantly.[18]

Central to self-giving is loving interpersonal involvement, essential to marriage, based on the generous giving of each spouse to the other. Each is available to the other for engaging in the basic project of life, which includes the task of growing closer to God. It is *personal availability*, not just the sharing of one's worldly possessions, that is primary. In that sense one can speak of self-gift without implying a loss

---

[16]Vatican II, *Church in the Modern World,* 48.

[17]John Paul II, "On the Family," Section 11.

[18]See Edward Schillebeeckx, *Jesus: An Experiment in Christology,* New York: Seabury, 1979, pp, 303-312.

of personal integrity. Each spouse, through sensitive listening and awareness, seeks to be more "present" to the other,
more welcoming of the other's entrance into one's own
affairs. Shared presence through openness, communication, and self-gift creates "we-territory," a concept developed in the writing of the French philosopher, Gabriel
Marcel.[19] Also writing in this same vein is Martin Buber,
who developed the classic statement of interpersonal philosophy in his work, *I and Thou.*[20] Buber noted quite percep-
tively that the same act through which one gains entrance
into the world of the "Thou," is also the act which creates
one's most true and significant self. Human life, in Buber's
terms, is vital only to the degree that one lives in openness
and communion with others.

Deep interpersonal involvement through love creates no
loss of personal autonomy.[21] In fact, such engagement is
necessary if one is to develop humanly to the level envisaged
by God in the risk taken by creating each person.

We become, therefore, more the kind of person God
intended us to be when we are most deeply related to others
in love. This may appear paradoxical within a philosophy
which values independence more than interdependence.
And it will appear simply as nonsense within a me-first
philosophy.

This description of Christian marital love rests on both a
capacity for genuine love, plus its enactment in a committed
marital relationship. If the relationship is genuinely personal, it will also be dynamic and active. It generates its own
history out of the possibilities brought to it by the marital
partners. The decision to unite in a common journey, or
separate into two distinct journeys is an option always
available within married life. Marriage does not require
common activity at every moment. What is shared is a
common intentionality, a common orientation through
which a married lifestyle is established.

---

[19]This is developed in Joe McCown, *Availability: Gabriel Marcel and the Phenomenology of Human Openness,* Missoula: Scholars Press, 1978.

[20]Martin Buber, *I and Thou,* New York: Charles Scribner's Sons, 1970, pp. 53-85.

[21]See Milton Mayeroff, *On Caring,* New York: Harper and Row, 1971, pp. 78-83.

Intentionality is a very difficult concept to define in objective terms because it lies more beneath the surface. It encompasses, however, what can be called the spiritual union of the couple. Throughout this chapter I have sought to protect the individuality or uniqueness of each spouse. In a healthy marriage, each one's uniqueness is, in a sense, guarded by the other. Kahlil Gibran said it well when he spoke about the need to allow spaces in togetherness — a space through which can blow the Spirit of God.[22] The poet Rainer Maria Rilke also recommended that the married do well if they safeguard each other's privacy. He invites them to embrace both the distance between them as well as their nearness. In describing married love he called it, ". . . the love that consists in this, that two solitudes protect and border and salute each other."[23] To employ another image, if trees grow too closely together they will not develop their full possibilities. Each will compete for the same nutrients, the same moisture and sunlight. In mental health circles, the concept of "psychic space" is used today to describe the need for personal room which allows one to maintain a sense of oneself, and of the possibilities of personal development. There is a need, therefore, for solitude even in the deepest of relationships.

A loving dynamism within the marital relationship also implies that each partner will be receptive to and welcome the inevitable changes which occur in the personal life of the other. Writings about marriage often note the need for adjustment, particularly in the first months or year of married life. It was commonly mentioned that the passage from the single state to married life was often difficult due to adjustments of lifestyle and to the accomodation of living with another person in intimate married life. While these perceptions are certainly correct, today's appreciation of changes occurring throughout the total life cycle calls for

---

[22]Kahlil Gibran, *The Prophet,* New York: Alfred A. Knopf, 1923, p. 15.

[23]Rainer Maria Rilke, *Letter to a Young Poet,* New York: W. W. Norton and Co., 1934, p. 59.

adjustments at practically every stage of personal and marital development.[24] What is needed as a component in marital love is a radical openness to the adjustment process. Marriage is much like the biological process of homeostasis; it oscillates almost continuously responding to both the minute and major interpersonal events which are occurring. Systems theory can be used to understand this process more clearly. In fact, one of the clearest indications that the common journey of marriage has really begun is that a fine-tuning is experienced in both wife and husband as each seeks to become more sensitive to the messages and wishes of the other. A sign that marital love is genuine is that these adjustments are not only accepted, but welcomed and performed with gladness.

The Presence of Unconditional Love

We are now touching upon what I would call the heart of marital love. I am referring to its quality of being *unconditional.* It is this feature of love which today causes much vexation among even well-intentioned people. To love without conditions sometimes appears close to being irrational.

We have all grown accustomed to living in a society which offers in most areas of life, a relatively high degree of predictability. We make plans for education or career with the general assurance that our plans will be realized unless some unforeseen event steps in. Should that happen, the obstacle is almost always interpreted as exceptional. We feel that if we prepare and plan well, success will generally be ours. The laws of the world, be they natural or societal, respond to our knowledge and our growing technological might.[25] This is what we expect and count on.

However, standing in almost direct contrast to our deal-

---

[24]The dynamics of marital life are discussed in chapter five.

[25]For the effects of economic hardship on a sense of control see Daniel Yankelovich, *New Rules: Searching for Self-Fulfillment in a World Turned Upside Down,* New York: Random House, 1981.

ings in the inanimate world of nature, is the world of interpersonal life. Many shudder at the thought of making a
lifelong commitment to another person, because there is
strong likelihood that the second person will change. It is
also quite possible that the first person will change. How can
anyone make plans on such an open future?

For many young people today the entrance to marriage
appears to be like a wide mountain crevasse which must be
crossed with an effort involving great risk. This risk is
lessened, it is believed, by acquiring a great deal of knowledge about the other person. But even this kind of familiar-
ity can only yield information about the past. The future will
always remain clouded in mystery. Some unmarried couples
decide to "live together" for a while in the hope that the
frightening risk of a lifelong promise will be lessened.[26]

There are also couples who marry without really thinking
about the distant future. They will stay together only as long
as "things work out." They incorporate into the marriage
agreement a significant conditional clause. Whether these
unions deserve to be called authentic Christian marriages is
debatable. My own view is that as much as there is absent
from their intention to accept the other "for better or
worse," to that degree the ensuing marriage will lack sacramental status.

What makes this situation all the more difficult is the
cultural setting in which we live. Very little substantial
support or value is given to long distance relationships.
While the newspaper will report couples celebrating fifty or
more years of marriage, there seems to be almost a quaint-
ness to these announcements. It is as if to say now we're
offering you a museum piece, something from days long
gone: a marriage which lasts fifty years!

Modern people, the jet-setters of our day, are in and out
of marriages like a change of clothes. No social stigma is
attached, anymore, to those who terminate marriage. The
event is not particularly applauded, but neither is it considered that much of a tragedy. It is something that just didn't

---

[26]Further discussion of this is offered in chapter four.

work out. Some jurisdictions now have laws which allow divorce simply upon signing a piece of paper. It takes five minutes.

This is not to claim, of course, that divorce is a simple matter. It remains for most a painful experience. The divorced often appreciate, more than the married, the value of marriage. Nevertheless, divorce rates are high, which indicates the difficulties encountered even by those who remain married. The point here is to note the social climate relating to marriage because it affects the possibility of couples entering marriage with unconditional love.

Another challenge facing marriage is the fact that people live longer today. At the turn of the century the average marriage in the United States lasted a mere fifteen years. Death, particularly of the wife, cut marriage short. Today, with the average life expectancy in excess of seventy years, the possibility of fifty-year marriages is no longer a remote prospect. When a person promises "until death do us part," ahead is the prospect of a half-century of marriage to one person. That expectation may appear rather ominous, especially in our era which experiences a rate of social and technological change unprecedented in human history.[27]

A Reflection of God's Love

Every genuine act of love in the world, in marriage or outside it, is also an act of God. This is not simply a pietistic wish. It corresponds to the pattern of understanding and activity revealed by Jesus. God acted through Jesus throughout his life. Those who encountered Jesus met in and through him the Lord God of all creation.[28]

The pattern of human and divine partnership was revealed as the pattern of all human activity. In being invited to wash the feet of others, to feed the hungry, and

---

[27]The nature of unconditional love as it applies to the changes during adult life is discussed in chapter five.

[28]See Edward Schillebeeckx, *Christ, the Sacrament of the Encounter with God,* New York: Sheed and Ward, 1963.

clothe the naked, all of us were alerted to the fact that for God's love to exercise its transforming effect in the world it requires human cooperation.[29]

While bringing God's presence and activity to bear on earthly events takes place through individual action, it often takes on more dramatic form when accomplished through communal endeavor. This relates directly and explicitly to marital life. We read in Genesis: "God created man in his image; in the divine image he created him; male and female he created them" (Gen. 1:27).

This intriguing passage suggests that the "imaging of God" preeminently occurs in the union of "male and female." Right from the beginning God's intent was to create within humanity "a pair" who are called in their togetherness to reflect God in the world. In this way God's nature, not so much as a God of power but as the God of Love, is disclosed. John Paul II pointedly captures this insight in his exhortation on family life:

> "God is love and in himself he lives a mystery of personal loving communion. Creating the human race in his own image and continually keeping it in being, God inscribed in the humanity of man and woman the vocation, and thus the capacity and responsibility of love and communion. Love is therefore the fundamental and innate vocation of every human being."[30]

Being created in the image of God means, at its deepest level, being made to love. No one is exempt from this calling. Perhaps the greatest tragedy of a human life is not to have experienced being loved, or not to have taken the risk of loving another. While Christian marriage is certainly not the only communal setting where love occurs, it is the primary setting for its enactment for those called to this state in life.

---

[29]Vatican II, *Church in the Modern World,* 3, 11, 12, 22, 32 and 38.

[30]John Paul II, "On the Family," Section 11.

If understood in the total setting of Christian thought, the theology of Christian marriage is closely related to the theology of the Trinity. On the surface the connection between God's own interior life and the community of marriage may not appear obvious. Part of the difficulty in appreciating the link between the two relates to a rather anemic view of God's Trinitarian life held by many. One of the first doctrines taught in early religious education is that of the Trinity. Young Christians were simply told that there is one God and three divine persons. Images of the three-leaf clover or the triangle were offered to assist the student in grasping the concept of three in one. Most children were satisfied with this explanation. After all, clovers and triangles are easy to imagine. This may, in fact, conclude any further thought about God's own life. No practical connections will be made between God's life and our own. Reflection on God will include that admission that God is a Mystery. The doctrine of the Trinity will remain something that Christians should know about, but after that, further speculation is left to theologians.

This scenario is unfortunate because within a theology of the Trinity are important insights which can illumine some of the primary mysteries of human life. For instance, to recognize that it is central to the very nature of God to live in intense community awakens us, created in the image of that same God, to pursue this in our existence. Also, the theology of the Trinity notes that the identity of each divine person is based on the kind of relationship each enjoys with the others. God the Father (or God the Parent, as some would prefer), is the "God of Origin" because the Son (or divine offspring) comes from the Father. This act of generation is continual; it has no beginning nor end. The Spirit springs (eternally, as well) from the others. They are welded together in deep love, a love which fully respects the uniqueness of each. There is genuine diversity which is maintained in each one's love for the others. Their love for each other supports their life together.

We are forced to use human language and images to converse in meaningful ways about God. What is important in this all to brief sketch of a theology of the Trinity is that God's life is a shared life, and this fact does not destroy or inhibit their life; it intensely enlivens God.

This same pattern is replicated in creation, particularly in marriage. As a primary community of love, wife and husband enliven each other, while at the same time their marriage gives witness to being rooted in God's very life. Basing a theology of marriage on a Trinitarian theology insures a proper emphasis on the unique persons in each loving relationship. This also allows the theology of marriage to be more effectively related to the mainstream of Christian thought.

Marital love is also established as the essential element in Christian marriage. It is objectively founded on God's own personal life. The married are called to love, to be like God, and to cooperate with God in the continued transformation of creation.

Christian marital love arises from within the relationship of wife and the husband as subjective expressions of each. But its total meaning transcends their subjective spirit. Objectively, it is founded ultimately in God. And further, their love for each other is not meant to remain solely within their mutuality, but like God's love, it is to be creative of new life, both in terms of children which might issue from their union, and from the other types of service they may render in the community.[31]

The totality present in marital love is appropriately expressed through the body/spirit composite which constitutes them as persons. Marriage is a social and sexual community. God made it that way. Marital sexuality is both a gift and a challenge. Because it is a critical dimension in marital love, it is part of the task faced all along the journey. Sometimes marital sex will be sustaining and supportive. At other times it may seem more like a restriction or a stumbling block. The teaching of the church concerning marital sexual love has vacillated from tolerance to strong endorsement. A reading of traditional treatises on sexuality may

---

[31]The generative aspect of marriage is discussed in chapter six.

give the impression that the church was intent on building retaining walls around this area of life. Today, a more apt image might be that of the church as sensitive teacher or bridgebuilder from the old to the new.[32] A consensus is growing within the church that marital sex must be approached with a new seriousness, with respect toward traditional values but with some new mapping depictive of its role in God's unfolding plan of love.

[32]This image is found in Dwight Hervey Small, *Christian: Celebrate Your Sexuality,* Old Tappen, New Jersey: Fleming H. Revell Co., 1974, p. 16.

CHAPTER III:
EXPRESSED IN SEX

Christian marriage creates a personal spiritual union between wife and husband. Yet, because they are enfleshed human persons, it is impossible to accomplish this without bodily involvement. So, what comes to mind, even within a discussion of their spiritual union, is how their sexual joining is part of their marriage. God has designed marriage as a unique type of union between enfleshed persons. According to the thought of John Paul II: "Conjugal love involves a totality, in which all the elements of the person enter — appeal of the body and instinct, power of feeling and affectivity, aspiration of the spirit and of will."[1]

Christian marriage is the most earthy of the sacraments of the church. Its distinctiveness comes from its direct link with the order of creation itself. While the Genesis accounts of creation carefully rule out the experience of sex as divine, they nevertheless appreciate it as among the many good things created by God. Sex is not elevated to a status above ordinary activity, nor is it degraded by listing it as a sub-human activity. The importance and value of sex is established by simply affirming it as part of the relational life of

[1]John Paul II, "On the Family," Section 13.

God's human creatures. Building on insight from the last chapter on marital love, human sexuality can powerfully remind us that we are created for each other as well as for God. Being sexual indicates dimly, yet significantly, that this relational side of human life is, in a real way, a reflection of God's own relational life.[2]

Body and Spirit Joined

This is the drama of interpersonal life. With the uniting of bodies, spirits are also knit together never again to be the same. When there is a genuine exchange of spirit, the body is also involved.

What has just been noted expresses an insight late in becoming a significant element in the thought of the church. For most of its life, the church was negatively influenced by a form of dualism originally popular in the secular philosophies of Ancient Greece. In general, the interpretation can be traced to Plato who espoused a sharp contrast between soul and body, the spiritual and the corporeal. Not content with simply affirming this separation, it also denigrated the corporeal by judging it evil, and sexual activity was thought to be most depraved.

The most influential theologian of the first millennium of Christianity, St. Augustine once embraced the ideas of a group called the Manicheans. They were strong devotees of a version of Platonic thought who held the material world and sexual relations in utter contempt. After his conversion to Christianity, Augustine felt the need to justify the goodness of sexuality against his former confreres. The best argument he found was that the goodness of sexuality came primarily from its role in procreation. Even in marriage, he believed, the use of sex had to be carefully controlled, and only engaged in for the sake of procreation. He once stated, "A man who is too ardent a lover of his wife is an adulterer,

[2]Walter Kasper, *Theology of Christian Marriage,* New York: The Seabury Press, 1980, pp. 26-27.

if the pleasure he finds in her is sought for its own sake."[3] In itself, Augustine found marital sex without value. It was too tarnished, in his view, by the destructive effects brought by the sin of Adam and Eve. The generative parts of their descendants would not obey reason, so if they must be used, it was only in marriage that it was allowed. This brought Augustine to further justify marriage on the grounds that it could be a remedy for concupiscence (the desire for illicit activity, particularly as it related to the sexual). Many centuries later, an Augustinian monk put together a similar definition of marriage. He called it a hospital for incurables. His name was Martin Luther. Marital fidelity allowed the couple a way of dealing with weakness.

What I have just described are Augustine's three "goods" of marriage: procreation, fidelity, and sacrament (which meant indissolubility — lifelong marriage was a sign of God's faithful love). Augustine's description of Christian marriage, and the role of sex therein, had enormous effect on church thought for many centuries.[4] Yet, given the intellectual and social climate of his era, credit can be given to him because he effectively saved the goodness of marriage from being swept into the philosophical negativism so common in his day.

Part of the cost of that victory was an uncritical acceptance of the meaning of sex as purely biological or corporeal. The possibility of appreciating a spiritual goodness in sex was impossible because widespread dualism (separation of body from spirit) remained a part of the philosophical thinking in the church for centuries. Marriages without sexual relations, the so-called Joseph-Mary unions, were valued as more saintly than those involving sexual intercourse. Augustine believed that the marital bond, when based totally on spiritual love, would be stronger and more stable than a love based on sexual exchange. The positive approach to marital sex, particularly as presented in the

---

[3] St. Augustine, *Against Julian,* II, 7.

[4] St. Augustine, *The Good of Marriage,* 6.

teachings in Vatican II, literally broke new ground and should now be viewed as the accepted view against which opposing views must be compared and evaluated.

What assisted the church to grow toward a more beneficial acceptance of sex was a gradual realization that the dualistic anthropology inherited from the Greeks, which viewed the body simply as a prison for the soul, was an inadequate explanation of the human nature. Human perceptions, feelings, thoughts, and desires cannot be reduced or compartmentalized simply as spiritual acts. They relate to and affect the total person.[5] If they are genuinely human, they will effect, either positively or negatively, both body and spirit. Humans cannot be disected into parts without killing the person.

The body and the spirit can be distinguished for purposes of discussion or analysis, but not described as operating independent of each other in reality. In that sense they are polar concepts, not opposites.[6] Some human experiences tend more toward being spiritual or corporeal. But we know of no experiences which involve only one or the other. The "body" and the "spirit" refer to two realms of human experience, and it is in accord with proper responsibility to render to each its due. This understanding of human nature is the foundation upon which sexual activity can be appreciated as always having a spiritual dimension.

On the other hand, sex is widely decribed in today's secular terms as simply a bodily response, an area to be researched, an activity with which to experiment, a way to "win friends and influence people." More and more the body is viewed instrumentally as a tool with which one "works." This approach puts a distance between the self and one's body. This violates the principle which states that I *am* my body, as distinguished from a view which states I *have* a body. Applied to sexual activity this results in a person "having" sex as one moves to describe in number and kind

[5]An excellent discussion on this is found in Maurice Merleau-Ponty, *Phenomenology of Perception,* London: Routledge and Kegan, Paul, 1962, pp. 186 and 269.

[6]I am indebted to Dr. James Walter, St. Meinrad School of Theology for bringing out this useful distinction.

the nature of one's sexual activity. Emphasis is placed on technique and performance with all concern being related to whether "it" is good or not.

In one sense contemporary society has not outgrown the imagined separation of body and spirit which victimized our ancestors. In its place we find a new kind of division or alienation: the separation of sex from the person, or, as it is more commonly portrayed, the severance of love from sex. Today's issue concerns sex being reduced through a type of depersonalization. Sometimes this travesty hides under the cover of assumed liberation. It can be debated whether, in fact, the solution offered to what was viewed as repression in the past is nowadays even more enslaving, or more of a misrepresentation of reality. The spread of vulgarity in almost every sector of society, and not at all limited to a particular gender, might also indicate the manner in which sex has been removed from significant personal concern to a level where "it" can be "enjoyed" without an accounting of how its actualization might affect the human spirit.[7]

Persons are not angels, and if there was a tendency in the past to fail in appreciating the earthy side of sex, it was a welcome change when attention shifted toward valuing sex as a significant aspect of human life. The Catholic bishops of Canada recently issued a paper on marriage which boldly expressed the following: "Our understanding of sexuality shapes our notion of marriage. Therefore, we need to examine the true meaning of sexuality in the order of creation, before we can speak about marriage and conjugal love."[8]

The former denigration of the physical is clearly giving way to a religious appreciation of the potential for creation to be revelatory of God. This is a very Catholic approach, which has maintained, often almost as a single voice among Christian churches, the conviction that God can be known from the imprint of divine causality and activity etched in

[7]John W. Dixon, "The Sacramentality of Sex," in *Male and Female*, edited by Ruth Tiffany Barnhouse and Urban T. Holmes, III, New York: The Seabury Press, 1976, p. 243.

[8]Canadian Conference of Catholic Bishops, *Marriage and the Family*, 1980, p. 85.

matter. The great Jesuit scientist/theologian, Teilhard de Chardin stated that we should praise and exalt material creation because it is that which "the Lord came to put on, save, and consecrate: *holy matter.*"[9]

Because spirit is in matter, and because many contemporaries have lost the sense of a spirituality related to those things which are so earthy in appearance, it is a real challenge to maintain a religious faith open appreciating the presence of both the spiritual and the material within the same earthy events.

It is also important to remember that the power inherent in sex should not be overestimated to the point that a pansexualism develops, where everything human is thought of in sexual terms. Sex is a dimension of human life. It is not the sole purpose for existence. Rollo May reminds us of the "diamonic" power of sex which he defines as its power to usurp the total self in a way that precludes the role and value of other aspects of human life.[10] While there is a crude example of this in what is termed "the free love" movement, as it is exemplified in the world of pornography, there is perhaps a subtle form of this present in those who employ cliches like: the all-pervasive presence of sex in life. Being present and being pervasive are not to be equated.

It may be granted that this type of exaggerated language is simply a reaction to those who fail to perceive a sexual aspect to anything except genital sexuality. Yet a view which sees sex in everything may be as distorted as the outlook which sees it almost nowhere.

Sexual identity impacts, however minutely, everything one thinks, says, or does, but in most things it is only a peripheral matter. John Paul II is quite correct in affirming that there are two different or distinct ways of "being a body" and this is relevant for grasping the significance of our God-inscribed identity.[11]

[9]Teilhard de Chardin, *The Divine Milieu*, New York: Harper and Row, 1960, p. 81.

[10]Rollo May, *Love and Will*, p. 123.

[11]As quoted in Joan Meyer Anzia and Mary G. Durkin, *Marital Intimacy: A Catholic Perspective*, Kansas City: Andrews and McMeel, 1980, p. 10.

Sex relates to both the body and the spirit. Both are dimensions of the sexual person. But if the focus is on the private self, it matters little whether one is woman or man. This is, perhaps, what is behind Paul's reference to the baptized where it makes no difference whether one is male or female. "All are one in Christ Jesus" (Gal. 3:28). In matters of relating to God, sexual identity is totally irrelevant. However when one considers relationships between humans the issue of sexual identity becomes markedly significant. In marriage, of course, sex is of critical importance because it distinguishes the marital community from all other social groups. So much of the quality of the marital relationship is determined by how the partners, as sexual persons, relate to each other. In the marital context, two issues deserve extended consideration. First, there is the matter of sexual equality. While this merits general societal examination, it has special meaning in marriage. Second, a major challenge is the manner in which their sexual activity becomes a genuine expression of love. To state this all somewhat differently, the basic issue for couples is the manner in which Christian love of neighbor is translated into sexual love of spouse. In order for genuine adult love to occur, fundamental equality between them must be there as a foundation.

Sexual equality currently remains an existential issue even in our so-called enlightened times. Clear thinking is necessary in this area before sexual love can be discussed. For without genuine equality, what may be called sexual love is nothing more than window dressing for what is probably sexual domination or servitude.

Sexual Equality

Common in treatments of this topic is a beginning which distinguishes between sexual role and sexual equality.[12]

---

[12]A recent publication spends 741 pages trying to argue that the retention of this distinction is central to Christian revelation. See Stephen B. Clark, *Man and Woman in Christ*, Ann Arbor: Servant Books, 1980.

Betrayed in such an approach is the very point discredited above: an artificial separation between matter and spirit. The rift here takes a different form by separating the person from the social structure in which that individual abides and acts.

To illustrate the correct understanding, notice how the progress made in women moving toward fuller participation in all realms of societal life relates decisively to the affirmation of full equality between women and men. Those who oppose feminine access to any area of the public sector in principle are guilty of sexism, and deserve to be labeled as such. John Paul II is quite clear in affirming freedom for both women and men in this matter. In his recent work on the family, he notes: "There is no doubt that the equal dignity and responsibility of men and women fully justifies women's access to public functions."[13] He goes on to note that this access should not be at the expense of the traditional roles of wife and mother. This is further nuanced by a reminder to husbands and fathers concerning the importance of their involvement in the family.

What we are seeing today is a dramatic shift in the basic structure of society which invites significant maturation on the part of both sexes. It is fruitless to debate who might be winners or losers. It can be a "win-win" situation for both if the pursuit of equality is accepted in freedom and understanding. This personal and societal transformation creates conditions which could result in a kind of development within marriage unprecedented in human history. As with all major societal changes, tension and confusion are inevitable. The roots of sexual inequality are deep. And it can be argued that a significant element of the words and deeds of Jesus concern the eradication of masculine superiority, particularly as it affects marriage and family life.[14]

A fascinating interpretation of male resistance to women's freedom is provided by Walter Ong, eminent inter-

---

[13]John Paul II, "On the Family," Section 23. See also Vatican II, *Church in the Modern World,* 29, 34, 52, 55 and 60.

[14]Morton T. Kelsey, *Caring,* New York: Paulist Press, 1981, pp. 90-91.

preter of social history, particularly as it touches religious sensitivities.[15] Ong argues that anti-feminism is based on male insecurity over personal power, especially as the male seeks to outstrip maternal controls embedded deeply within the psychic substratum. Male anxiety over being judged as possessing feminine traits causes him to assert a total separation from the female and brings him to affirm clear male competency in most areas of life. The females in society, on the other hand, are more comfortable in appropriating male prerogatives and style, although this is done with slight modifications. Sexuality seems to imprison men more than it does women. This is not to say that men cannot move to that level of maturity, one which accepts full equality with women. It remains, however, a real challenge, and confronts men today with one of their most difficult and serious undertakings. Overcoming male dominance, or "machismo," is a necessary requirement for insuring a marital relationship based on the equality inherent in God's creative intent. The words of John Paul II are worth quoting at length in this regard.

> "Authentic conjugal love presupposes and requires that a man have a profound respect for the equal dignity of his wife . . . As for the Christian, he is called upon to develop a new attitude of love, manifesting toward his wife a charity that is both gentle and strong, like that which Christ has for the Church."[16]

The idea of sexual equality is not new. Scripture interpreters identify its presence in both creation accounts in Genesis. This is particularly interesting given the assumed absence of that idea in the tale of Adam's rib, at least, as it has been interpreted through the centuries. Readers of English translations of the Bible are often given a false impression when woman is identified as a "helpmeet" (KJV), or as

[15]See Walter J. Ong, *Fighting for Life: Contest, Sexuality and Consciousness,* Ithaca: Cornell Univ. Press, 1981, pp. 69-74.

[16]John Paul II, "On the Family," Section 25.

a "helper fit for him" (RSV), or as "a suitable partner" (NAB), although the latter rendering is the best of the three. None of them captures, however, the original Hebrew which is more aptly translated "someone alongside him" or "corresponding to him." In the original is found the notion of similarity, accompanied by a sense that similarity does not mean total sameness. For each other, woman and man become genuine counterparts. As they face each other, each can see something of a true reflection of oneself.[17]

Over the years theologians have struggled with the Genesis account, perhaps knowing in their hearts that some sense of equality had to be drawn from the texts. St. Bonaventure, a major theologian in the Middle Ages, provided an explanation which may appear somewhat quaint today, but probably caused a significant stir among his contemporaries. He wrote:

> "Man and woman, according to the nature and properties of their respective sexes, were so made that they might be united to one another and thus have rest and support in and through each other. Because, therefore, man and woman are joined to each other by a strong and singular bond (*forti vinculo et singulari*), one sex was produced from another. Because that union gives man rest (*dat viro quietationem*) the woman was taken from man while he slept. Because a man is a woman's strength and support it is said that the woman was made from his bone. And because in all these things there is a certain equality in a shared society (*quaedam aequalitas mutuae societatis*), the woman was then not from any old bone, but from the man's rib and from his side."[18]

While equality may be affirmed in theory, another way in which the relationship between the sexes may be distorted is

[17]See Stephen Sapp, *Sexuality, the Bible and Science*, Philadelphia: Fortress Press, 1977, pp. 12-15 and Gerhard von Rad, *Genesis: A Commentary*, Philadelphia: Westminster Press, 1961, p. 80.

[18]Quoted in Fabian Parmisano, "Love and Marriage in the Middle Ages," *New Blackfriars* 50 (1969), p. 605.

through establishing predetermined role descriptions which allow little room for the uniqueness enjoyed by each marital partner. The last chapter outlined the manner in which mature love requires the self-standing wholeness of each partner. Mutual integrity is necessary for a love relationship to be sound. Love seasoned in that way was termed "gift love." It was distinguished from "need love." In gift-love significant personal breakthrough occurred as one stepped out and entered the world of another person. This same act of self-transcendence is central to any realistic portrayal of personal enrichment in marriage. If the marriage partner is simply used as an instrument for self-enrichment, what results is not growth, but regression. If the partner is more an object of worship or veneration, interpersonal distance is perpetuated preventing quite effectively the type of mutual exchange ideally found in marriage.

While the struggle for sexual equality is occurring on virtually all fronts of society (and the struggle may best be viewed as akin to the contractions of the birth process), nowhere is it more focused or intense than in the wife-husband relationship.

Our language is undergoing needed revision, and our awareness of the many contexts where sexual equality is at issue will require on-going sensitization. A sense of inequality may be hidden in the notion of complementarity between the sexes. A concept like complementarity has to be analyzed to determine whether it is really a mask attempting to cover a sense of personal inadequacy, particularly as it is focused on the identity of the woman. Commonly accepted portrayals of marriage, like "two in one flesh" or "a boy for you, a girl for me," will have to be analyzed to ascertain what is really being affirmed or denied.

This is already being done in many sectors of societal life. Yet, the context of that inquiry appears, on the surface at least, to be largely limited to the area of the political or economic order. What has to be kept in mind is that sexual equality is also a religious issue. With God expecting so much from the marital relationship, responsibility demands that nothing be taken for granted, particularly if it is central to marriage as is the need for full equality between the partners.

We have assembled, so to speak, the basic ingredients of marriage. Standing before each other are two fragile human beings, equal before God and each other, capable of gift-love particularly as it can be expressed in the sexual union. Marriage provides the structure for their joining together as co-participants in each other's life journey. Merged is nothing less than their personal lives, which is symbolized uniquely and pointedly in their sexual embrace.

Over the centuries the formal teaching of the church has vacillated on how it wants to evaluate, locate, or accept the role of the sexual encounter in marriage. In general this particular act of love was accepted, although at times a better word for describing the church's view would be toleration. The church seemed more at ease in accepting the spiritual aspects of marriage. Marital sex was generally approved, but it was largely because of its effect in producing offspring. The spirit and the body were understood mostly as parallel aspects of being a person; the process of their integration was hardly imagined.

It is good advice to be cautious and skeptical of prophets announcing that the new day has arrived, but here, largely due to Vatican II, we are both blessed and burdened with an opportunity for creating new possibilities in joining body with spirit. Possessing a better philosophical framework in the church, a more intelligent response to the body/spirit unity can be expected. This new opportunity is probably due to the manner in which discussion of marriage and sexuality in the church has involved the wisdom and experience of Christians who are married. They bring to the church a unique gift built around the intimacy of marriage, family, and the home.

Sexual Intimacy

In an often overlooked passage from Vatican II is found the text which suppresses any view of separating body and spirit. The passage reads: "By their very nature, the institution of matrimony, itself, and conjugal love are ordained for the procreation and education of children, and find in them their ultimate crown."[19] Love generates life. Older formulations of this would have referred to the biological union of the spouses as generative of life. The newer description acknowledges a more comprehensive meaning of marital sex, a meaning which includes both the spiritual and the corporeal. It also sets the stage for affirming a much closer linkage between sexual relations and the totality of marital life. In the past arguments for restricting sexual intercourse to marriage rested primarily on the relationship of sex to procreation. While that approach remains correct and should not be disregarded, the now accepted, more comprehensive meaning of sex creates other considerations.

Sex in marriage expresses in corporeal word the depth and range of the relationship already existing, as well as the direction toward which the relationship is developing.

For the sake of honesty and authenticity, the word of the body should genuinely exhibit the attitude of the spirit. Because all language requires both honest telling and faithful hearing, it is not sufficient to simply speak without providing evidence that one's words are true from other areas of life. Sexual words are only part of the marital language.

Each marriage will both receive a language from history, and create a new language unique to the particular couple. As their relationship develops, they will creatively form new words and gestures. The various elements of their sexual interchange, if genuinely a part of their actual marital relationship, will become more personal and special to the particular marriage.

Being in touch with the deeper levels of the marital relationship, and being able to express that depth in bodily form, is quite a challenge. Given the way sex has been reduced in meaning by association with relatively shallow areas of life, for instance, in its being exploited to sell

[19]Vatican II, *Church in the Modern World*, 48.

commercial items (the girl in the bathing suit on the hood of the new car or the baseball player in underwear), it is probably true that this natural link between the interior and exterior has, for many, been severed or weakened. Sex so often and so tragically is quite prone to being depersonalized.[20]

Sexual love can be viewed as somewhat of an untamed force within the person. Its power can have significant, positive effects within a relationship, prompting a kind of awareness and concern for another, hardly possible through any other means. To use the words of Charles Davis, sexual love is capable of causing "a man or woman to give up everything for the person loved . . . "[21]

What marriage provides for sexual love is a setting in which the fullest meaning of that kind of love can be protected, directed, and enhanced as it relates to ever fuller dimensions of the wife-husband union. Sexual love is not necessarily the most altruistic or generous expression of love within marriage.[22] In fact, there can be occasions in marriage when the suppressing of sexual activity is the most loving thing to do. In times of sickness, during times when sexual abstinence is required to prevent procreation, or simply when the act would be more an effort to use or abuse the spouse, it may be better to "remain silent sexually" or to use other, non-sexual expressions of affection and concern.

The basic questions of Christian marriage are always the same. How does this particular wife and husband honestly enrich and enliven the love between them? How do they express in body what is present in the spirit? How can all the physical expressions of love best serve the developmental needs of the total love relationship of the marriage?

The body can attend to the spirit, or it can block what is

---

[20]See Rollo May, "Reflections on the New Puritanism," in *Sex: Thoughts for Contemporary Christians*, edited by Michael Taylor, Garden City: Doubleday and Company, 1974, p. 171.

[21]Charles Davis, *Body as Spirit*, New York: The Seabury Press, 1976, p. 129.

[22]See John Giles Milhaven, "Conjugal Sexual Love and Contemporary Moral Theology," *Theological Studies* 35(1974), p. 698.

inside from seeing the light of day. Sometimes such hindrances cannot be helped. Victimized by personal history there are those who have been taught that the body is evil, or that sex is unbecoming. It may be that individuals have been brought up to be defensive, secretive, or private. Feelings are not to be shared. Thoughts are not to be disclosed. Yet, for those individuals and marriages afflicted by these blockages, there often develops other ways through which the body expresses the spirit. That is why, as was already noted, each marriage will create its own "best way" or unique language to express what's genuine for that particular relationship. The special characters of each marriage must be both protected and respected in view of the uniqueness each person possesses before God and others.[23]

The process through which mature and generous sexual love comes into being is an essential part of the formational aspect of marriage. In a legalistic or static description of marriage, so characteristic of church language in the past, the quality of marital sex as a genuine expression of love was hardly alluded to, much less valued. Now, however, with center stage in the theology of marriage given to the dynamic process of developing love, sex is valued as an important ingredient of that love. Christian marriage encompasses potentially everything which flows between wife and husband. The task of breaking down barriers, whether natural, cultural, or even brought about by sinfulness, constitutes the lifelong charge offered the couple by God. The many dimensions of marital sex: work and play, reward and cross, comfort and affliction, all express and contribute to the overall vitality of marital love exchanged as the fabric of a particular marriage is knit together. Sexual activity can symbolize and make more tangible what might be only hinted at in other ways. Love between persons can be expressed in countless ways, but marital love finds in the full sexual exchange a word most appropriate. Other words simply cannot say it as well.[24]

[23]See Rosemary Haughton, *The Passionate God*, p. 292.
[24]Stephan Sapp, *Sexuality, the Bible and Science*, p. 127.

This is because sexual intercourse allows both to enter bodily into what is most private and personal in the other. Revealing to each other in naked encounter the gift each is for the other, sexual activity disarms each person, creating a degree of vulnerability inappropriate in any other relationship. Again, no one has to be reminded that this does not always happen. The sexual act can be trivialized or used to state meanings less than that associated with the gift of self. But exceptions need not be taken as denying the ideal. Rather, what is possible and most appropriate in marriage needs to be held up for those who can and will follow its direction. Mutual interpersonal exposure, with idiosyncrasies and peculiarities intact, protected, and cherished through the full lifetime of the marriage, suggests a meaning for sexual love which identifies all lesser settings outside marriage as verging on the paltry or empty.

It should also be mentioned that no one is ordinarily revealed fully in a single act. The process of self-exposure, the revelation of the self and not just the physical body, is what is being described here. While a single act of sexual intercourse is perfectly capable of generating a child, the generation of the marital relationship by means of the sexual encounter is more exacting and cannot be accomplished in a single act. The process of Christian marital growth will include then, as one of its salient features, the sexual aspect of conjugal life as it flows from the unique loving exchange of wife and husband.

When boredom or conflict color their sexual encounters, Christian wives and husbands should look for ways to reinvigorate this aspect of their marriage. There are skills to learn and perfect. The human sciences have developed useful insights which can help many couples especially through the guidance of knowledgeable and sensitive counselors. In many cases, what can help relates to the integration of the diverse elements within marriage, the sexual, the psychological, the economic, the religious. Integration is a primary task in adult life. All enter adulthood with many unassembled individual pieces of a puzzle. The adult years provide the opportunity for arranging the pieces into a unified whole. The same can be said about the marriage relation-ship. It begins with many areas of attraction, but time will be needed for the relationship to reach totality. The process of relational integration can be both painful and exhilarating.

With each marriage established with the prospect of a long future, another unique consideration of our epoch is the value and the task of maintaining long term sexual intimacy. We know from studies that a full sexual life is biologically possible well into the so-called golden years. If sex is, in fact, a gift from God, it is to be used both joyously and responsibly. Pulpits should ring with this message, although that may be too much to expect. It is well to be reminded of Thomas Aquinas' condemnation of the vice of *insensibilitas*: the failure to allow ourselves the appropriate sensual enjoyment which comes as part of God's good gifts in creation.[25] In various experiences of personal and com-munal life, in eating and drinking together, and in the enjoyment of sexuality, one's openness to enjoy and give thanks for these pleasures, implicitly gives honor to the one who made it all possible.

Sexual experience in marriage can be accompanied by a type of freedom unavailable in any other setting. While worries related to a possible pregnancy are sometimes all too real, or even concern about something as mundane as the uninvited interruption by small fry, married couples can rest in that trust and security which flows from the marriage commitment, made and honored, which forms an abiding backdrop to daily life. Each can "let go," knowing of the good will and love of the other. Awkwardness can be laughed at; an all-thumbs approach to love-making can be forgiven. The spirit of playfulness can enter the bedroom.

It is regrettable that church talk about these matters, at least in the past, seemed more bent upon control or repres-sion, than of inviting the spirit to break forth in bodily

---

[25]Thomas Aquinas, *Summa Theologiae*, II-II, 142, 1. See also Herbert W. Richardson, *Nun, Witch, Playmate: The Americanization of Sex*, New York: Harper and Row, 1971, pp. 26-36.

ecstasy. Little was heard of celebrating God's gifts when they possessed an erotic aspect.

The rather off-handed and sensuous way in which the Song of Songs celebrates marital sexual love stands in sharp contrast to typical discussions of sex among church moralists. Today there is widespread acceptance of the fact that when Scripture, particularly in the beautiful document of love that the Song of Songs is, describes the beauty of breast and body, it means what it says. Centuries of Christian scholars rejected that rather literal (and earthy) meaning because it was thought to be beneath the dignity of God's inspired word. Human sexual love, they argued, was simply a metaphor for God's love of us. Before his martyrdom in a Nazi death camp, Lutheran pastor and theologian Dietrich Bonhoeffer noted the special appropriateness of the Song of Songs being included among the sacred writings because they serve as a protest against those who would assume God's rejection of human passion.[26]

Fortunately, the advice given by Origen, a third century Christian writer, to readers of this sacred book is no longer considered appropriate. In his lengthy commentary on the book, he included this cautionary note:

> "...I advise and counsel everyone who is not yet rid of the vexations of the flesh and blood and has not ceased to feel the passion of his bodily nature, to refrain completely from reading this little book and the things that will be said about it."[27]

This attitude of repression and control runs deep in the history of Christian thought. Clement of Alexandria, a predecessor of Origen, who with others defended marriage against the elitest Gnostic groups which saw no value whatsoever in sex, still recommended restraint. He advised that if

[26]Quoted in William E. Phipps, *Recovering Biblical Sensuousness*, Philadelphia: Westminster Press, 1975, p. 66.

[27]Origen, *The Song of Songs: Commentaries and Homilies*, Ancient Christian Writers, Vol. 26, Westminster, Maryland: Newman, 1957, p. 23.

marital sex had to be done, it should occur only at night-time. Origen in a similar vein asserted that the Holy Spirit was always with married Christians except during sexual intercourse where it would not be fitting for the Spirit to be present.[28]

To effectively counter these negative approaches, what gradually developed in the church was a positive theology of creation. Included quite explicitly in that theology was the affirmation of humans created as sexual persons. This resulted in reformulating a beneficial theology of marital sex. My own theological approach begins by asserting that God created the earth alive with love-energy, but needed human cooperation to release it into interpersonal life. The reservoir was full, God was most generous in gracing the world with divine love. But if it is mistakenly believed that matter is fundamentally opposed to spirit, or that earthly events operate in competition with God's activity, opportunities will be by-passed for releasing God's love-energy in the world. What is needed, therefore, is an awareness of the endowment God invested in creation and a human willingness to cooperate with God's intent.

In his message on the family, John Paul II uses this type of approach in presenting his thinking on artificial contraception. His argument is based more on the nature of interpersonal dynamics, than on the more traditional approach founded on natural law. The Pope writes:

> "Thus the innate language that expresses the total reciprocal self-giving of husband wife is overlaid, through contraception, by an objectively contradictory language, namely, that of not giving oneself totally to the other. This leads not only to a positive refusal to be open to life, but also to a falsification of the inner truth of conjugal love, which is called upon to give itself in personal totality."[29]

[28]Origen, *Homilies on the Book of Numbers,* 6. Quoted in Joseph Martos, *Doors to the Sacred: A Historical Introduction to Sacraments in the Catholic Church,* Garden City: Doubleday and Co., Inc., 1981, p. 408.

[29]John Paul II, "On the Family," Section 32.

Given the personalistic foundation present in his thought, the philosophically-oriented Pope appears concerned toward respecting the full created potential of marital sex. It represents an orientation sensitive to the overall dynamics of a graced creation which includes the erotic experiences of marriage.[30]

This also builds a foundation for affirming the sexual pleasure in marriage which is appreciated as something willed by God, a benefit of God's generosity. Andre Guindon, esteemed Canadian theologian, notes that when pleasure is not found in human activity it may be a sign of estrangement from what is most suitable in the person. Something is not in harmony with the vibrancy of creation. He also recalls that Thomas Aquinas discusses the issue in the broad context of God's desire to share beatitude which comes as a natural outcome in being faithful to our natures as created.[31]

Though it may seem more theoretical, bodily ecstasy may be appreciated as part of the effects of the Resurrection of Jesus, now shared in the world. Rosemary Haughton's exciting theological treatise, *The Passionate God,* outlines a way Christians can search for the effects of redemption, particularly as they may be present in experiential form.[32] Her thesis is that the power and presence of the divine is often to be found within the adventure of romantic passion and love. In that type of experience, a breakthrough can occur exposing the person to a level of life unnoticed until then. Since God's love for us is passionate, it is fitting that moments in human life reflect this. God's love creates new possibilities within human experience, first in Jesus himself, then among those who are drawn into sharing his life. Those possibilities are personal, involving both spirit and body. Just as God took flesh in Jesus to make love more real in

[30]See Penelope Washbourn, "The Religious Dimensions of Sexuality," *Christianity and Crisis,* 34(Dec. 9, 1974), p. 282.

[31]Andre Guindon, *The Sexual Language,* Ottawa: University of Ottawa Press, 1976, p. 72.

[32]See Rosemary Haughton, *The Passionate God,* pp. 46, 58, 82, 154, 172, 194 and 259.

human form, that same love is still active transforming created love in human history. What is particularly promising about Haughton's insight is its application to the loving experiences of ordinary people. With a deeper appreciation of the interrelation of spirit and body a more holistic recognition of God in ordinary human experience can develop. A tantalizing vision of how the experience of passion relates to God's love affair with humanity is also suggested.[33]

Although it may appear as unlikely, or at least paradoxical to pre-Vatican II thinking about marital sex, there now seems solid arguments to propose that the more deeply material, earthy, or enfleshed marital life becomes, it becomes more, not less, spiritual! This also supports a new argument for the inclusion of marital sexuality as an essential element in identifying Christian marriage as a sacrament.[34] As wife and husband accompany each other on life's journey, they express their shared life uniquely in acts of uniting their bodies along the way. Sex expresses the warmth and depth of their love, the personal affirmation each offers the other.[35] And in this way, a further activization of their relationship with God is occurring. Bernard Lonergan, often esteemed as the most influential North American Roman Catholic theologian of this century, describes this process as the joining of horizontal finality (the union of the spouses) with vertical finality (their union with God).[36]

With the sexual aspect of marriage receiving the approval of God (which was always there) and the church (a more recent endorsement), it is perfectly appropriate for married couples to seek to improve the quality of their sexual relationship. In secular bookstores are found many works offering detailed blueprints for realizing one's sexual potential.

[33]*Ibid.*, p. 287.

[34]The sacramental meaning of Christian marriage will be developed more fully in chapter eight.

[35]Mark Mogilka, "Models, Levels and Possibilities of Sex in Marriage," in *Enriching Your Marriage*, edited by Robert Heyer, New York: Paulist Press, 1980, p. 83.

[36]Bernard Lonergan, "Finality, Love, Marriage," in *Collection*, New York: Herder and Herder, 1967, pp. 29, 37, 48 and 50.

Sometimes these books are called marriage manuals, or to borrow a note from the best-selling books of Alex Comfort (*Joy of Sex, More Joy of Sex*), they are gourmet recipe guides to sexual love-making. They give the impression that there are pre-existing models of "perfection" which deserve imitation. Given the sales of these types of books, many couples probably feel somewhat inadequate in sexually expressing their love and affection for each other. Marital sex, like human language in general, can always improve. Yet overuse of expert opinion, or an attempt to be like someone else, may result in a dead end for married couples.

A more appropriate approach would begin with the uniqueness of each couple and their marriage. While open to the good advice of others, primary concern is more related to pleasing each other. As mutual knowledge and appreciation grows, they will be open to include expressions of affection and support which flow from their marital relation. Love becomes more "home grown." They establish, in somewhat unprecedented fashion, what God's love can mean when transformed into Christian marriage. While one's own marriage will be known by others, and can serve as a model, it will always possess features that cannot be translated because each marriage, if authentic and healthy, will be unique because of the unique husband/wife relationship. No individual marriage deserves to be slavishly imitated by others. There are no "perfect" marriages.

This underscoring of uniqueness makes a significant religious point as well. In the creation accounts of marriage, recorded in the first few chapters of Genesis, no archetypal marriage is offered as an ideal. No mythical prototype couple, divine or human, is offered as a pattern for others to imitate.[37] Each marriage establishes anew what God intends for marriage. What is right or appropriate for each marriage arises directly from within that marriage. The unique personality, gifts, and talents of each marital partner contribute toward forming a "once and for all" love relationship. This

[37]See Joseph Blenkinsopp, *Sexuality and the Christian Tradition*, Dayton: Pflaum Press, 1969, p. 25.

principle also contributes to the degree of freedom and responsibility experienced by the married. What is chaste and proper for each depends on the nature of their relationship, and each one's uniqueness as a person before God. General guidelines relating to honesty, integrity, generosity, sensitivity, decency, and kindness are both appropriate and necessary. Good guidance is also needed from the church as it interprets God's word. Philosophies of sexuality which degrade the individual or which relate to only a part of the person deserve condemnation. So also are those views which trivialize the sexual aspect of human life. Sensitivity to the moral dimension of sexuality in marriage is an essential part of the general moral fiber of marriage. Sexual exploitation is just as possible within marriage as it is outside it.[38]

A Christian understanding of sex will appreciate its role as central to the dynamics of the love between wife and husband. Catholic teaching sees it as "an integral part" of their love and, when expressed apart from that context, it is nothing more than a lie, a falsification of one of God's most treasured gifts.[39] Respected theologian, Bernard Haring notes that one of the great tragedies of our time relates to the way sexuality is distorted in some contemporary settings. He writes that sexual misuse results not from its being overemphasized, but rather, in its alienation or separation from genuine love.[40]

When sex is an expression of genuine marital love it has tremendous positive power. The acknowledgment of marital sexual love as symbolizing God's love for us should induce a serious consideration of all aspects of married life. Loving sexually is a way of grasping something of what happens when God's disturbing, yet attractive presence enters human life. It invites us to admit that there are

---

[38]David Mace, *The Christian Response to the Sexual Revolution*, Nashville: Abingdon Press, 1970, p. 132.

[39]John Paul II, "On the Family," Section 11.

[40]Bernard Haring, *Free and Faithful in Christ*, Vol. 2, New York: The Seabury Press, 1979, p. 509.

surprising ways in which God can be revealed in creation, one of those ways being through the sexual expression of love between wife and husband.[41]

To account fully for the place of sex in Christian marriage, its presence will be alluded to in settings besides acts of sexual intercourse. More and more there is an inclination to affirm a sexual facet in all the significant exchanges between wife and husband. This has led to speculation that sexuality contributes something to human language particularly as it operates in intense social encounters. While "sexual language" can be expressed in many social encounters, it is most influential in the marital relationship, where the full range of sexual language is appropriately expressed, and the deepest level of human interaction can be experienced.

Human sexuality, in general, nurtures sensitive and intimate exchange. It can uniquely express compassion, support and a depth of feelings hardly expressible in any other way. Through sexuality, humans are endowed by God with both a reminder and a power to accomplish that which is most important in life: the act of love.[42] This point has been developed extensively in the addresses and writings of John Paul II. He sees in the created structure of woman and man a "nuptual meaning." This meaning is "marked" in their bodies. In a public audience, early in 1980, he stated the following:

> "The human body, with its sex, and its masculinity and femininity, seen in the very mystery of creation, is not only a source of fruitfulness and procreation . . . but includes right 'from the beginning' the 'nuptual' attribute, that is, *the capacity of expressing love in which the man-person becomes a gift — by means of this gift — fulfills the very meaning of his being and existence.*"[43]

[41]Charles Davis, *Body as Spirit*, p. 130.

[42]James B. Nelson, *Embodiment*, Minneapolis: Augsburg Press, 1978, p. 8.

[43]John Paul II, *L'Osservatore Romono*, Jan. 21, 1980.

Implied is the fact being created as woman or man indicates an orientation toward love, a predisposition in harmony with human nature as given by God, to express oneself in love through heterosexual engagement. This approach extends significantly earlier theological thought, held widely in the Catholic tradition, that sexuality points exclusively to a procreative meaning. While recent advances in church teaching do not deny this, it emphasizes another aspect of sexuality: its meaning in relation to one's loving capacity. In fact, since all are created either women or men, this newer meaning signifies a *more fundamental* understanding of sexuality, particularly if the Christian context is considered because of the value ascribed to the vocation of permanent celibacy.

Conjugal love is also creative of life. Love creates life and new life is created to love. The cycle of God's own life is reproduced in human form in Christian marriage. Marital affection is love made whole through bodily expression. "This [marital] love is uniquely expressed and perfected through the marital act."[44] So it was written in the documents of Vatican II.

Yet almost two thousand years before, the apostle Paul penned quite similar thoughts.

> "You must know that your body is a temple of the Holy Spirit, who is within — the Spirit you have received from God. You are not your own. You have been purchased, and at a price. So glorify God in your Body . . ." (1 Cor. 6:19,20).

[44]Vatican II, *Church in the Modern World*, 49.

CHAPTER IV:
CELEBRATED IN RITUAL

Weddings are big business. If a moratorium on weddings were declared, florists, jewelers, photographers, renters of formal wear, caterers and musicians would all suffer a significant decrease in business. But this is unlikely because the celebration of the passage from the single life to marriage is observed by ceremony and festival now and, as far as human memory has it, has always been a part of the events which mark this passage of life. Formal celebration and ritual sensitizes the community to those incursions of special meaning which establish the peaks and valleys of life. Without festivity, all days appear as equal, which usually means that they slip into dull routine. Events of birth, death, arrival, departure, plus those occurrences which significantly alter a person's status in the community, are lifted out of "ordinary time," and inserted in a "time of their own." No known human society exists without celebrational rituals. They vary from culture to culture in type and form, and can be approached like ciphers or windows through which the main values of a given society are most apparent.

The church values ritual in singular fashion because it serves to establish vital contact with the divine source of its life. The sacraments of the Roman Catholic Church designate critical moments of religious development and transition. They express in concrete form the perceived dynamics of God's life when most available within the community. Serious concern for the *quality* of the church's rituals indicates sensitivity to a central dimension to religion based on the principle of incarnation: a belief that God acts in and through terrestrial events.

When Pope John XXIII called for a redefinition of the relationship of the church to the modern world by convening Vatican II, it was most fitting that the first area of church life to be considered for revision was its liturgical life. An important insight is found in this strategy. In the liturgy Catholics experience their church concretely with an impact unlike any other area of personal religious activity. It is not surprising that those Catholics who resisted reform, along with those who supported it, fought their skirmishes first over issues relating to liturgy. And while the intensity of that conflict has lessened today, a careful scrutiny of church life still shows evidence of continuing debate.

This wrangling is not necessarily unhealthy because it indicates that the liturgy of the church remains close to the center of people's religious life. If no one cared, there may be a kind of peace. Yet, this would also suggest an unhealthy resignation which is only appropriate as a prelude to death.

Religious ritual is tied to life. When healthy, it gathers space and time, people and things, and fashions them all into a shape symbolizing the richness of life when blessed by God. The gesture of living ritual captures human events, and positions them in a framework which exposes their roots divine and deep, while allowing a nurturing of growth unparalled in prosaic, ordinary activity.

Good liturgy will be different, not so much in the content of what is done, but through the spirit in which it is accomplished. Explicit prayerfulness is allowed to permeate events. They are set in "a Divine Milieu," to borrow a phrase from Teilhard de Chardin.

To designate an area of human life as sacramental is not to change it into something else, but to acknowledge and celebrate its existing sacred status. Naming an event sacramental does not deny its humanness. In fact, the opposite should happen. Through the Incarnation of God in Jesus, God's love and acceptance of humanity warrants the sacredness of *this* world. This fact is celebrated whenever Christian liturgy takes place. Christian sacraments are not actions which launder a dirty world, but are gestures of gratitude to God for establishing this world as bathed in grace through creation and the forgiveness of sin. The redemptive act of God sets the tone for religious response in liturgy as one of gratitude. In thanksgiving the community pledges that it will work to become even more holy.

Reflection on this fact is necessary to overcome a tendency which has plagued Christianity almost from its beginning. Weak religious belief often vacillated on whether the world was really sanctified by the Christ's coming. Like the hopeless gambler who puts money on all possible outcomes, individuals often thanked God for all that God had done, and then allocated resources for influencing God just in case God was capricious in generosity. This is, no doubt, a major religious issue and it cannot be adequately discussed here. Yet if we are to view the sacraments as Christian gestures of celebration and thanksgiving, a clear appreciation of the religious context in which these celebrations take place is necessary.

While the world is saturated with grace, there are certain moments, certain stages in the journey of life, when the community of belief needs to open ourselves to that fact. An ancient principle of sacramental theology is that sacraments are for us, not for God. They orient us in a way that is most aligned with the situation and direction of life established by God.

Sacraments are, therefore, not magical activities which exist apart from the awareness and attitudes of those who participate in them. God guarantees available power and value, but the "state" of the community and its members can seriously block or depreciate this. Personal and communal preparation is necessary to gain all that is available within the ritual celebration.

Participants more conscious of what is taking place, and more committed to the relational values being celebrated,

will be more enriched through the sacramental happening.[1]
In the words of Vatican II:

> "But in order that the sacred liturgy may produce its full
> effect, it is necessary that the faithful come to it with
> proper dispositions, that their thoughts match their
> words, and that they cooperate with divine grace lest they
> receive it in vain."[2]

Another feature of the sacraments is their role in providing that divine assistance needed by Christians to live the
full life intended for each person by God. The demands of
the Kingdom are strenuous. The first disciples of Jesus are
often caught in the Gospels wondering aloud over how
anyone might respond to Jesus in the way he advocated. The
tradition of the church described sacramental grace as that
special help from God which assisted the community's
response by word and deed in those areas of life addressed in
each particular sacrament. God's help is comprehensive,
although we seem to need the assurance of specific aid
available in certain areas. In Christian marriage, with its
requirements of fidelity and exclusiveness, which is no small
order particularly in contemporary society, sacramental
grace flows from God's promise that no one will be tempted
beyond a capacity to resist. And while the cross will be part
of Christian marital life, it will be, in the words of Scripture,
"sweet and light."

Sacramental rituals "shape" and "direct" God's power
toward sectors of life which might be viewed as precarious
or dangerous. Announced within the sacramental rite is the
welcome word that we are not alone in our struggles to
accomplish good. Sacraments are, therefore, moments of
accountability, both for ourselves and God. Many of the
sacraments signal the beginning of new states in life. One
function of the sacramental ritual is to take into account

[1]James M. Schmeiser, "Marriage in Contemporary Society," *Eglise et Theologie*
5(1974), p. 102.
[2]Vatican II, *Constitution on the Sacred Liturgy*, 11.

personal resources as a new journey is begun. Sacraments provide a push in the right direction as well as a reminder that, while we are expected to use all our resources in accomplishing the goal, our efforts are supplemented by God's own assistance. They are not occasions for complaining about personal inadequacies, but celebrations which express gratitude that we are not required to bear any burden alone.[3]

Entrance into the new state of marriage significantly alters identity, role, and lifestyle. New expectations are created by oneself, one's spouse, and the community. God's help is guaranteed. Whether the community offers its resources will depend on whether the need is seen, and whether there is a willingness to allocate resources for the purpose of assisting couples in responding to the demands of Christian marriage. Official church mandates are clear in advocating this assistance, but general directives are more easily made than an allocation of concrete assistance and programs.[4]

The ritual of Matrimony expresses a particular time in a special setting, the intentions and desires of two hope-filled Christians to share their lives as wife and husband. It is a significant love-event celebrated in the midst of the local Christian community. While the ultimate source of their love is in God, the couple can take pride in their willingness to direct a significant portion of their response to God's love toward their wife or husband. Matrimony takes a general, nonspecific love of neighbor and intensely focuses it upon a specific person. This is not idolatry, but an application to the concrete world of God's passionate love for the world which is boldly made real in the world of everyday life.[5]

It should be obvious that if God's love is to be made real on the face of the earth, it will happen oftentimes in the

[3]See John W. Dixon, "The Sacramentality of Sex," in *Male and Female: Christian Approaches to Sexuality*, edited by Ruth Tiffany Barnhouse and Urban T. Holmes, III, New York: Seabury Press, 1976, p. 248.

[4]John Paul II, "On the Family," Sections 65-75.

[5]Karl Rahner, *Foundations of Christian Faith*, New York: The Seabury Press, 1978, p. 399.

joining of wife with husband. It would also appear as fairly logical that the celebration of their love in liturgical ritual would be part of the ordinary sacramental activities of the church. Yet, a brief trek through the history of the church reveals that the celebration of Christian marriage, for the first thousand years of its life, was not considered a major part of the church's ritual life.

Institutional endorsement of Christian marriage needed the development of a positive theology of marriage. Practice and theory are not separable. Our present liturgy of marriage (and the many customs which accompany the celebration) are the product of a long history. Understanding some of the key elements of that history can provide both a grasp of the developing theology and an appreciation of today's ritual. It will give those approaching their wedding a better understanding of what they will do, thereby making their experience of the event more meaningful and effective. For those already married, an understanding of the path taken by history can illuminate some of their own experience of Christian marriage. It is an application of the principle "ontogyny recapitulates philogyny", that the history of the individual reenacts the history of the whole. The struggle of the church to develop an adequate theology of marriage, along with a sacramental ritual which satisfactorily expresses that theological vision, is also a struggle within each marriage to understand and express the fullness of all that is going on, particularly as God sees it. The theological task of each person is to take all that has been revealed by God, and see it happening in personal life. With regard to marriage, the church found this to be problematic. Once marriage was accepted as both sacred and sanctifying, however, a precious resource was exposed. This process of discovery is still going on.

A History of Matrimonial Ritual

Over the years, the church's reflection on the various aspects of Christian marriage reveals both the complexity of marriage itself, and the divergent values marriage embodies. Overall, the church has sought to defend marriage against its detractors, and with pastoral care, promote marriage as a relationship quite within God's intent for humanity. Always in the background of any historical survey, one must keep in mind the peculiar character of each epoch to prevent a misinterpretation of the intentions of the church. This also means that part of the task of constructing a positive and useful theology of marriage for today demands a sensitivity as to what assailed and what assisted Christian marriage in each period of history. This creates a balanced approach which brings forth wisdom gained from history and joins it to a critical reflection on the contemporary situation. This reflection also helps to determine what is worth eliminating because it is no longer appropriate, and what is worth saving because it is part of the lifeblood of Christian marriage

A HISTORY OF MATRIMONY

We are fortunate in having good historical surveys describing the evolution of the church's approach to marriage, as well as accounts of marital customs as they developed, particularly in the West.[6] A brief survey of these findings is offered here to illustrate the rather laborious process through which the church gained a more comprehensive and positive theology of marriage. It should also be noted that the process is ongoing, and while the breakthroughs accomplished by Vatican II are certainly significant, they should in no way be viewed as the last chapter of the book. Further, much of this development has occurred in the

[6]For further information consult: Joseph Kearns, *The Theology of Marriage*, New York: Sheed and Ward, 1964; John Noonan, *Contraception: A History of its Treatment in Catholic Theologians and Canonists*, Cambridge: Harvard University Press, 1965; Joseph Martos, *Doors to the Sacred: A Historical Introduction to Sacraments in the Catholic Church*, Garden City: Doubleday and Co., Inc., 1981; Paul Palmer, "Christian Marriage: Contract or Covenant?", *Theological Studies* 33(1972), pp. 617-665 and Edward Schillebeeckx, *Marriage: Human Reality and Saving Mystery*, New York: Sheed and Ward, 1965.

cultural setting of what is usually termed Western Civilization. Significant insight into broader meanings of Christian marriage may be anticipated once other cultural matrices are allowed to develop and articulate the experience of marriage. Of particular interest will be developments from Sub-Sahara Africa and Oriental cultures of the Far East.

Our reflection begins where it must with the New Testament period. Jesus, while not recorded as having addressed the issue of marriage to any great extent, took a strong position in support of the marital relationship in the few passages we do have on the topic. He apparently did not accept the current views on divorce and remarriage available at the time. What he stated was this: "Whoever divorces his wife and marries another commits adultery against her; and the woman who divorces her husband and marries another commits adultery" (Mk. 10:11-12). Supporting this rather absolute position was Jesus' view that marriage was not only a matter of the union of wife with husband (he refers to Gen. 2:24), but also a relationship having God as its active creator. "Therefore let no man separate what God has joined" (Mk. 10:9). Jesus invited his listeners to look at marriage in a new framework as a particular relationship subject to God's active involvement in its creation and continuance.[7]

Elsewhere in the gospels (Mt. 5:28) Jesus reformulated the issue of adultery as not only involving a physical act, but also interior attitudes and thoughts. Marriage for Jesus involved the total person. Legalistic categories, although important and certainly widespread in Jesus' time, could not match the depth of meaning he associated with marriage. Jesus might even be interpreted as poking fun at human attempts to regulate or define the sacred relationship of marriage. He was also concerned about justice and personal rights in marriage. He assigned no privilege to either the woman or the man in marital matters.

---

[7]See Wilfrid Harrington, *Mark*, New Testament Message, Vol. 4, Wilmington: Michael Glazier, 1979, pp. 152-156.

Later church practice seems to have altered the original view of Jesus, as in the adding of the so-called "exception clauses" recorded in Matthew and Luke. Jesus himself referred to the founding intent of God for marriage, and the direction implied in it. Marriage was designed by God as a relationship of two people bound together for life. This was not an impossible vision, although neither was it necessarily easy.[8] The church is both blessed and burdened with the so-called hard sayings of Jesus. The church immediately attempted to pastorally translate the views of Jesus into the practical life of its members.

In the years following the Resurrection and Pentecost the primitive church was charged with implementing the Gospel. The exception clauses, for instance the gospel of Matthew, allowed for divorce in the case of "lewd conduct" (Mt. 19:9). This might refer to marriage attempted between those having close ties of kinship. Scholars debate the point. Most agree, however, that the reference is not to simple adultery, an unfortunate error in some translations. The Greek word for the exception mentioned, *porneia*, is not easily translated because it could refer to a variety of situations: general immorality, incest, etc. The "exception" cases do serve to show, however, the strains within the church to apply the apparent intent of Jesus in a literal way.

We also have information about marriage in the letters of St. Paul. In some of the early local churches many wondered whether good Christians should marry, remain married, or remain single. In the air was the belief that the second coming of Jesus was close at hand. This expectation formed the climate for Paul's advice to these new Christians. He personally advocated the life of celibacy as best, and qualified his remarks by noting that he was speaking particularly for himself. He was not proclaiming a general teaching of Jesus. In matters as sensitive as whether one should marry or not, Paul left each person with the freedom to decide what was best. He, therefore, concluded: "I have no desire to place restrictions on you, but I do want to promote what is

---

[8]Divorce will be discussed more fully in chapter eight.

good, what will help you to devote yourselves entirely to the Lord" (1 Cor. 7:35). Advocacy is in the realm of freedom. Support is rendered in accord with the calling each person receives from the Lord.[9]

In the first three centuries of the church, marriage was simply approached in a matter-of-fact manner. Christians married according to family and local custom. There were no church ceremonies for marriage. Occasionally it was judged necessary to defend the goodness of marriage against certain Gnostic sects which opposed marriage. We also find occasional condemnations of sexual licentiousness, which apparently was quite common in seaport towns along the Mediterranean coast. There are also intermittent denunciations of divorce. In general, however, the church was rather silent about marriage. In homilies and other catechetical material, marriage was simply accepted as part of God's good creation. Support was based on references to the creation accounts in Genesis and by noting the presence of Jesus at the wedding feast of Cana.[10]

In the fourth century we find a gradual emergence of what might be called paraliturgical rituals associated with marriage. A special blessing was locally offered to clerics who married. Bishops charged with the care of orphans often "blessed" their marriages. Weddings for the most part, however, were still enacted in the customary settings of family or local community. One noteworthy advance was the church's recognition of the marriage of slaves, something not acknowledged by the Roman civil authority. About this time we also come across marriage blessings in local collections of rites, although it is difficult to determine their usage. It should also be mentioned that these blessings are almost

[9]See Jerome Murphy-O'Connor, *1 Corinthians*, New Testament Message, Vol. 10, Wilmington: Michael Glazier, 1979, pp. 58-76.

[10]It is interesting to note how often in the Christian tradition the Cana episode was used to validate marriage from a Christian perspective. A careful reading of this incident in John's gospel reveals little, if anything, about marriage itself. Except for possible eschatological overtones associated with "the wedding feast" at the end of time, what really happens is more related to the symbolic importance of what takes place in relation to that famous water.

exclusively for the bride. Parenthetically, the tradition of blessing only the bride was not changed until the liturgical reforms mandated by Vatican II. The liturgy now includes blessings for both the bride and the groom.

About this time there also developed the beginning of separate approaches to marriage in the East and in the West, between Constantinople and Rome. In general the Eastern approach to marriage developed in a more wholesome fashion. The strong sense of legalism and unacceptance of the sexual side of marriage, so significant in the West, was relatively absent in the East. Marriage was more easily appreciated in a spiritual framework. Greater emphasis was given to the role of the priest, so much so that to this day, the priest is viewed as the primary minister of Matrimony. By the fifth century, the practice of crowning the bride during the wedding developed in the East. Also part of the ritual was the priest joining the hands of the bride and groom, a custom formerly reserved for the father or guardian of the bride. The East also maintained a less rigorous approach to divorce and remarriage than was the practice in the West, although a second marriage was not given the same meaning as the first marriage.[11]

Returning to the West, St. Augustine, the main theologian of marriage for most of its history, noted that one of the "goods" he saw in marriage was its character as sacrament. For him, this referred to the way marriage signed or symbolized the covenant relationship between Christ and the church. What's noteworthy about this fact is that except for Augustine's passing reference, marriage was not identified as sacramental until seven centuries later when Peter Lombard listed marriage among seven *special* "sacramentals" of the church.

From the seventh to the twelfth century there was a gradual, yet consistent development of church blessings which, in the beginning, were offered in addition to the civil procedures done according to local custom. In Western

[11]Edward Schillebeeckx, *Marriage: Human Reality and Saving Mystery*, pp. 344-356.

Europe as the early Middle Ages dawned, a gradual decline of civil authority took place in the secular realm. This breach of rule was filled by the institutional church which gradually accepted almost total responsibility for governing the social order. Concern over marriage impediments, validity of marriages, and other issues relating to matters formerly decided by non-ecclesial authority, now fell to church officials. In 866, Pope Nicolas I described a marriage ritual which took place entirely in church. He added, however, that participation in a church wedding was not mandatory. Couples, because of poverty or other difficulties, were permitted to exchange their vows in private.

Alongside its developing interest in marriage, the church also continued to value the state of virginity, appreciating it as the form of Christian life analogous to martyrdom. Canonization, formally limited to those who gave their blood as witness to their total dedication to the Lord, was extended to virgins, who were also venerated for their total consecration to God's service. The practice of veiling the bride, which came into use during this period, was probably thought of as being similar to the veiling involved in the ceremony for the consecration of virgins. In seeing and appreciating both the differences and similarities between the consecrated state of virginity and the married state, the church was gradually moving toward a more comprehensive theological appreciation of *both* states.[12]

Late in the ninth century, forged documents (termed "the false decretals of Isadore") entered ecclesiastical discussion supporting the extension of church authority to many areas of life. It was claimed that this collection of writings dated back to the Patristic Period. Many were purported to be decrees of popes and, while eventually branded as counterfeit, for awhile they supported further efforts to extend the authority of the church in civil matters, marriage included![13] In general, however, the extension of the church's jurisdictional power deserves a benevolent interpretation. Western

[12]*Ibid*, pp. 305 and 311.
[13]Joseph Martos, *Doors to the Sacred*, p. 423.

Europe was in disarray after the so-called barbarian invasions, leaving the restoration of the remnants of order and education largely to the church.

Problematic, nevertheless, was an ecclesial takeover of all sectors of life allowing for the possibility of confusion of the role of the church, particularly the clergy. Besides his growing role in spiritual matters, the priest also became a judge over many significant areas of life.[14] For marriage this meant that by the eleventh century virtually all marriages were under church jurisdiction and presided over by a priest. In some places the priest even blessed the wedding chamber at the conclusion of the day's festivities.[15]

In 1215, the Fourth Lateran Council prohibited clandestine marriages in order to protect those who might be forced against their will into marriage. Pastoral and legal concern became focused on the quality of consent between bride and groom, which was almost universally accepted as the most important feature of marriage. Supporting the emphasis on marital consent was the discovery about this time of the ancient legal code of Justinian which emphasized the mutual consent as the primary element in establishing a marriage. Opposition to the consent theory of marriage came from the law faculty of the University of Bologna, who argued that actual sexual intercourse established true marriage. Supporting the so-called *consensus* theory was the faculty from the University of Paris. It was not until a respected canon lawyer, Alexander III became pope that the issue was settled. He taught that a true marriage would exist simply based on mutual consent (like the marriage of Mary and Joseph). Such a marriage could not be dissolved by human agency. The church, however, had the power to dissolve the union if sexual intercourse had not taken place. For the church, sexual intercourse was viewed more as a completion or a cementing of the relation. Not even the church, according to the Pope, had the power to sever the

[14]Michael D. Place, "The History of Christian Marriage," *Chicago Studies* 18(1979), p. 316.

[15]Joseph Martos, *Doors to the Sacred*, p. 426.

bond established in a marriage that was *ratum* (ratified) and *consumatum* (consummated). One exception was made, however, through the use of the Pauline privilege, a case when a non-Christian marriage could be dissolved should one of the partners convert to Catholicism. What is important to note here is that many of the "ground rules" for dealing with marriage and divorce were established by the church as early as the thirteenth century.

Accompanying the growth of church concern over legal matters relating to marriage was a discussion of the meaning of marriage from a theological perspective. The development of an improved theology eventually complemented the expansion of church authority in marriage. We find then, as has already been noted, the listing of marriage as a sacrament of the church by Peter Lombard in a collection of works called *The Sentences*, which became a standard reference work for theologians in this very fertile and exciting period of theological development in the thirteenth century. An interesting, although not surprising, aspect of theological thought at that time was a belief that marriage was only a sign of God's grace. Christian marriage itself did not cause grace. Without going into great detail, it appeared that the church had problems in affirming the sacred nature of marriage because it included sex. To be a cause of grace meant than an act possessed essential goodness; it could be a means through which God acted. To ask this of marriage in the thirteenth century would be to request more than was thought possible at that time.

The church soon found itself, however, in the role of defending sexuality and marriage against the Albigensians, a major heretical sect quite widespread in France and Spain. The sect, sometimes called the Cathari, were quite Platonic in spirit, denigrating the goodness of the body because it was thought to be the prison of the soul. They were closely akin to the Manichaeans, who forced Augustine, almost a millennium earlier, to defend much the same issue.

Leading the opposition against their teaching was St. Dominic, himself, who eventually founded a religious order for the express purpose of converting of the Albigensians.

The Order of Preachers, as it was called, was also the community from which arose the most significant theologian of the Middle Ages, St. Thomas Aquinas.

While Aquinas wrote comparatively little about marriage, he contributed significantly to the theology of marriage, noting that the sacrament of marriage involved not only the consent of the marriage partners, but impacted upon the whole marriage. He emphasized the role of the marital bond which existed through the whole lifetime of the marriage. Theologians of lesser stature than Aquinas would subsequently see the bond primarily in terms of a legalistic meaning. The great doctor of the church, however, understood the bond quite comprehensively. The sacramental gift of God's grace was related to the bond of love. Marriage, for Aquinas, was a community of nature transformed by God into a community of graced life.[16] Aquinas, therefore, accepted marriage unequivocally as part of the sacramental life of the church.[17] Along with Albert the Great, Aquinas also affirmed that Matrimony was a cause of grace. He argued that God could not require sanctity in marriage without also supplying the means to achieve it.

John Duns Scotus, soon after Aquinas, described marriage as a contract between the spouses with corresponding rights, major among them being the *jus ad corpus*, the right to the body of the spouse primarily for the purpose of procreation. His approach does not merit being judged as a high point for the theology of marriage, yet his emphasis was quite influential for later church thought.

On the positive side, however, he was the first theologian to note that the true ministers of the sacrament of Matrimony were the bride for the groom and the groom for the bride.[18] This insight brings to a close developments in the

---

[16]Thomas Aquinas, *Commentary on the Fourth Book of the Sentences,* Questions 26 and 27.

[17]Thomas Aquinas, *Summa Theologiae,* III, 65. A summary of Aquinas on marriage is found in Edward Schillebeeckx, *Marriage: Human Reality and Saving Mystery,* pp. 325-343.

[18]See Martos, *Doors to the Sacred,* pp. 433-434.

theology of marriage for the next few centuries. Both in terms of theory (the accepted theological description of Christian marriage), and in practice (the ritual and customs associated with the wedding), what existed at the close of the thirteenth century remained fairly intact until Vatican II. There were minor increments; for instance, the Council of Florence in 1439 officially listed Matrimony among the seven sacraments and noted it not only symbolized the presence of grace, but also caused it to come to the married couple. The Council was merely including in official church teaching the existing theological consensus established by the great Scholastic theologians.

The Council of Trent, in 1563, noted that the sacramental grace of marriage perfected the natural love of the couple and strengthened the indissoluble unity inherent in the marriage bond. That Council also taught that sacramental grace assisted in the sanctification of the spouses.[19] What is most remembered from Trent, however, was the requirement that Catholics marry according to a specific form: in the presence of a priest and two witnesses. To quote the decree from the Council:

> "...even though it cannot be doubted that clandestine marriages, made by the free consent of the contracting parties, are valid and true marriages, nevertheless...this Holy Synod declares null and void the contracts of those who attempt to marry in any other form than before the pastor or another priest...and two or three witnesses."[20]

The decree sought to negate an argument of certain humanists to limit or discredit the authority of the church. Historical awareness of marriage customs and rites prior to the tenth century, performed without church involvement, provided the reformers evidence needed to undermine existing church practice. The church, they claimed, should not be

[19]Council of Trent, Session 24.
[20]Council of Trent, *Tametsi Decree.*

involved in purely civil activities. Marriage is solely a matter of secular concern. No doubt, there were existing abuses of ecclesiastical power which added fuel to the reformers' arguments.

The Council responded not by limiting church power, but by extending it. The historical context for the position taken by the Council of Trent sheds light on why it acted as it did.

When the position of Trent was formally inserted in the official law of the church a canon was added which allowed for marriages to take place without the prescribed "canonical form," where local conditions rendered implementation impossible. An interesting aspect of implementation was that it was only gradually applied throughout the world. In the United States, for example, the decree was promulgated only in the provinces of New Orleans, San Francisco, parts of Utah, Vincennes, and St. Louis. In the rest of the United States, before 1908, it was possible to contract marriage without a priest and the marriage was judged as valid.[21]

It should also be mentioned that the concern of the Council of Trent was to draw into the public sphere marriages which in the past may have been clandestine. Christian marriage was regarded not simply as a private agreement between two individuals; it had significant effects both in the *civil* or *secular* community and in the building up the life of the Church. Whether the bishops at the Council of Trent were aware of these multiple dimensions is unknown. It can be said, however, that the inclusion of marriage in the public life of the church is theologically important because the vitality of marriage effects the overall strength of the church. What follows next is a consideration of why it is most appropriate to celebrate marriage in the communal gathering of the church.

THE CHURCH WEDDING

For centuries Christians married either privately or in the company of family and neighbors. We saw that a marriage

21Bernard Siegle, *Marriage Today*, (2nd Edition), New York: Alba House, 1973, p. 198.

ceremony was only gradually introduced into the formal environs of the church, and for reasons perhaps more related to the civil than religious order. Yet, there exists no evidence that Christians failed to appreciate a religious meaning to marriage. Marrying "in the Lord" meant that Christian couples took to heart the implications of being a Christian as it related to ordinary marital and family life. Pastoral care was extended to the married and, while there may have been undeveloped or even deficient views concerning the meaning of sexuality in marriage, whenever philosophies arose denigrating either sexuality or marriage the church was immediate in defending both as part of God's intended creation.

We have already discussed the historical process through which Christian marriage was accepted as an important part of church life. While the church's concern for marriage may appear, on the surface at least, to be almost entirely juridical, there coexisted in the tradition of the church a body of important literature which regularly drew upon images drawn from marriage. I refer here to accounts of the spiritual life, descriptions of spirituality and prayer, which often used nuptial imagery to describe the deepening of a personal relationship with God. Unfortunately, these discussions of spirituality were often kept apart from formal theology, a separation which only recently is being overcome. Christian theology in the Patristic Period knew of no separation between spirituality and theology. But gradually formal theology broke into many specializations and, while it would take us too far afield to describe this process, it should be noted that no disparaging judgment need be cast on Christian marriages in the past simply because formal theology had little to say about it. Another story can be told which is buried in what might be called the more informal literature of the church: personal histories and autobiographies of individuals, couples, and families who embodied in simplicity and depth the loving dynamics of the Christian life.[22]

---

[22]Besides the work of Rosemary Haughton, *The Passionate God*, other theological works which touch on this theme are John S. Dunne, *The Reasons of the Heart: A*

By including marriage in church life, both theologically and formally (which is a positive aspect of Trent's decree), the wedding event inaugurating marriage is dignified and identified as significant for the church as a social and public body.

On the human level the celebration of the wedding, with the public stating of the marriage vows, serves to impress both the individuals directly involved and the community at large that what is transpiring is not an ordinary event. It is tacitly stated that the effects of marriage are not limited to the private life of the particular wife and husband. New social roles are entered with concommitant responsibilities for the couple and the community. The human community is reshaped because those who were once two are now, in a real way, one. It would be naive for a couple to attempt a defining of their relationship without reference to the community. Individual social relationships fit into a larger pattern or web of social connections. Society is sometimes described as a "system" where, like a biological ecosystem, all the parts of the system are interrelated. A change in one area of the community creates effects throughout the total system.

The more a society understands the dynamics of its own life, the more it can effectively deal with the changes it constantly experiences. The public recognition and celebration of marriage serves to alert both the couple and the community to the *fact* of their interrelatedness. Celebrations expressing joy and satisfaction launch the couple's life, hopefully with the support of the community. On the other hand, when wedding festivities are clouded by worry or disappointment relations with the community are strained and what follows may not be the kind of support the marriage needs to prosper. Our rituals have a way of telling the truth. They allow certain facts to come to the surface.

Even more must be said when considering the celebration

Journey into Solitude and Back Again into the Human Circle, New York: Macmillan, 1978 and John Shae, *Stories of God: An Unauthorized Biography*, Chicago: The Thomas More Press, 1978.

of marriage within the Christian community, the church. Vatican II clearly dispelled any idea that membership in the church can be considered a *passive* activity. It began its description of the church with reference to an important biblical image, the People of God. Full emphasis was given to the fundamental value and dignity of every member in the church regardless of his or her status or role within the church. Each person brings a unique contribution to church life, which means that the church will be effective only to the degree that it supports and facilitates that full participation proper to each one's gifts and talents.

For Christians who are married, much of their "contribution" to church life will flow from their being wife or husband, mother or father. These roles do not exhaust their offerings to the life of the community, but they do qualify all that is given because of the way marriage and family life changes personal identity. When married, personal spirituality and ministry within the church community manifests a particular style or form. A church in touch with the grace and power of the sacrament of Matrimony will be enriched more significantly than one which views marriage and family life as inconsequential, or even worse, as a distraction from church life. A healthy church respects the uniqueness of all its members, downgrading none, appreciating all.

What does all this mean for the celebration of the wedding of a Christian couple in church? A comparison with the sacrament of Baptism will help. The celebration of Baptism indicates that new life is being brought into the community. The baptized person becomes a vital cell of the church in general, and the local community, usually a parish, in particular.

The liturgical celebration of Christian marriage also recognizes the creation of newness in the church. A "domestic church" or "church in miniature" is being formed. This new ecclesial community, formed by the married couple, ought not to be thought of as insignificant to church life because of its size. On the contrary, because the marital relationship contributes directly to the most basic quality of the church, its life of love, it should be acknowledged as the most basic community within the church.[23]

Further, as the church grows in understanding that its primary role is to live out and proclaim the love of God in and to the world, Christian marriage will properly advance to an ever more esteemed place within the life of the church. John Paul II, in his treatise on the family, forcefully set the tone for this type of thinking. Referring to how Christian marriage embodies the basic message of God's love, he writes: "... The central word of Revelation, 'God loves his people' is... proclaimed through the living and concrete word whereby a man and woman express their conjugal love."[24] Their love is creative of church life. This is the special gift of the married; it is their extraordinary charism.[25]

As evidence of recognizing their importance to each other and to the church, the couple itself is the minister of the sacrament. The presence of the priest or other designated religious witness is ancillary, not primary. The power of God, active with and in the sacramental ritual, flows through wife to her husband and through husband to his wife. This interchange initiates a process, a spiritual movement of reciprocity, which forms a pattern existing from the wedding "until death do us part." This grace-filled activity, made real through the interaction of wife and husband, cannot be over-emphasized. For each other, the spouses are truly instruments of God's life and love. The role of being minister of the sacrament establishes one's role in contributing to the spiritual perfection of one's spouse. It forms the bedrock upon which an adequate theology of marital spirituality and ministry can be erected.[26]

What then is the role of the priest during the marriage liturgy? Is he simply present for the legal assurance that all is done according to the guidelines of the church? And what

[23]Walter Kasper, *Theology of Christian Marriage*, p. 31.

[24]John Paul II, "On the Family," Section 12.

[25]Walter Kasper, *Theology of Christian Marriage*, p. 38.

[26]This will be developed more thoroughly in chapter seven.

about the two witnesses required by church law? Is there more to their presence than a role of honor coming from being selected as "maid of honor" or "best man"?

First, remember that we are searching for the religious meaning of the celebration. Valid and worthwhile human meanings, while important in themselves, are more fully grasped if integrated with religious meaning. In true sacramental fashion, the goal is to blend and relate all valid human or earthly meanings with their deeper, divine significance. From a cross-cultural analysis of marriage rituals it might be noted that a "third-party" presence is almost universal. By its very nature, therefore, marriage appears to require broader social involvement, a wider presence, which suggests an almost super-personal dimension to this earthly event.[27]

The presence of the priest and two witnesses, the "form" called for by the Council of Trent, may best be understood as representing a pastoral or religious support for the couple. Through these official witnesses the couple speaks to the community, and through the witnesses the community expresses the challenge it lays before each marrying couple. The community needs marital love for its own survival as a vibrant Christian community. It needs the living witness of married couples to both awaken and animate the community to the possibility of deep and lasting love. In its turn, the community is obliged to help the couple in the all too precarious task of living with and for each other in all that life will offer in the days and years ahead.

As much as possible, the wedding should, of course, be a personal statement of the marrying couple. Recent developments in liturgical guidelines allow much more flexibility in planning the ceremony. Readings can be selected from a broad list of possibilities. Processions and prayers can express the personal intent and style of the couple. Most of all, the marriage vows or promises ought to articulate with

[27]See Georg Simmel, *The Sociology of Georg Simmel*, New York: Free Press of Glencoe, 1950, p. 130.

precision the nature of the marital consent each is express-ing to the other. They must also contain the essential elements which comprise a Christian marriage.

But what are these essential elements? What specifically ought the wife and husband promise each other at the beginning of their marriage? These questions relate to the very nature of marriage as Christian, and in today's pluralistic and secular world it cannot be presumed that couples seeking marriage in the church will come "ready-equipped" with the attitudes and values proper in a Christian understanding of marriage.

Fortunately, some of the answer is already available. It is embodied in existing formulae now used within the church wedding ritual. According to present practice, any of the following forms may be used.[28] Also, without altering the essential points in the "packaged" vows, the wording can be modified to express a more personal statement by the couple. The first suggested form is this: "I, *N.*, take you, *N.*, to be my wife (or husband). I promise to be true to you in good times and in bad, in sickness and in health. I will love you and honor you all the days of my life."

Another accepted form, more traditional in style, available in dioceses of the United States, is: "I, *N.*, take you, *N.*, for my lawful wife (husband), to have and to hold, from this day forward, for better, for worse, for richer, for poorer, in sickness and in health, until death do us part." A clear understanding of these words is necessary so that the ritual exchange will not be "just words".

THE MARRIAGE VOWS

The fundamental theme of the marriage vows is the unconditional promise to love one another under all conceivable circumstances. The goal is the creation of an intimate community of life and love which is the basic

---

[28] *The Rites of the Catholic Church*, New York: Pueblo Publishing Co., 1976, pp. 541-542.

definition of Christian marriage according to Vatican II. During the wedding, each partner must intend this result. Whether each possesses the capacity for effecting this outcome can only be known in the days which follow. The promises of marriage are, to a certain extent, precarious and uncertain. It is not enough simply to hope for or desire that one's promises will be fully translated into life. The distinction between a realistic capacity for achieving an intimate community of life and love and simply a hope accompanied by no real ability to bring it about has been used in the determination of marriage annulments for those seeking such decisions from the official courts (tribunals) of the Roman Catholic Church. Of course, the definition of Christian marriage now accepted in the church is a vast improvement over earlier formulations, largely because of its strong personalistic spirit. Yet it is not easily used in making juridicial decisions. The definition of Christian marriage now relates to many areas of life because it touches not simply the joining of will or bodies, but the uniting of personal lives as well.

Germain Lesage has attempted to help in formulating some of the qualities required to create a genuine Christian conjugal community. He believes that a serious lack of any of these qualities could be grounds for assuming a potential inability to meet the goal promised in the marriage vows. Here is Lasage's list.

1. Oblatory love, which is not simply egoistic satisfaction, but which provides for the welfare and happiness of the partner;

2. Respect for conjugal morality and for the partner's conscience in sexual relations;

3. Respect for the heterosexual personality or "sensitivity" of the marriage partner;

4. Respective responsibility of both husband and wife in establishing conjugal friendship;

5. Respective responsibility of both husband and wife in providing for the material welfare of the home: stability in work, budgetary foresight, etc.;

6. Moral and psychological responsibility in the generation of children;

7. Parental responsibility, proper to both father and mother, in the care for, love, and education of children;

8. Maturity of personal conduct throughout the ordinary events of daily life;

9. Self-control or temperance which is necessary for any reasonable and "human" form of conduct;

10. Mastery over irrational passions, impulses or instincts which endanger conjugal life and harmony;

11. Stability of conduct and capability of adapting to circumstances;

12. Gentleness and kindness of character and manners in mutual relationships;

13. Mutual communication or consultation on important aspects of conjugal or family life;

14. Objectivity and realism in evaluating the events and happenings that are part of conjugal or family life;

15. Lucidity in the choice or determination of goals or means to be sought jointly.[29]

Also part of this issue is the shift from viewing Christian marriage as a contractual relationship to one of being a covenantal union.[30] When the bishops at Vatican II discussed marriage in the modern world they consciously and

---

[29]Germaine Lasage, "The 'Corsortium Vitae Conjugalis': Nature and Applications," *Studia Canonica* 6(1972), pp. 103-104.

[30]This will be explored again in chapter eight when we discuss those elements in Christian marriage which make it sacramental.

courageously departed from the longstanding tradition which viewed marriage largely in terms of contract, rights, privileges, and responsibilities. While Christian marriage retains elements of exchange based on justice, it also includes, or more precisely, embodies elements of love patterned after the type of love God has for each person. Vatican II opted for that deeper vision of Christian marriage.[31] While the language of contract may be more useful from a secular standpoint, the language of covenant is more appropriate from a biblical or Christian perspective.[32] Contracts are the cement of purely human agreements; covenants properly join God with people. With Christian marriage designed by God to reflect a divine covenant, it is more properly defined as a covenant relationship. Contracts also tend to be more impersonal because they cover the exchange of goods and services, whereas covenants involve agreements between people particularly where the persons themselves become the substance of the alliance. The virtue of justice operates to insure contracts; the virtue of love and fidelity guarantees covenants.[33]

An absolute opposition between what might be called "covenant reasoning" and "contract reasoning" could be misleading. It might also misrepresent the total exchange that is operative within Christian marriage. It is worth remembering that when the language of contract began to be used in the church, it was to insure the freedom of consent which established marriage. In marriage today, elements of

---

[31]See Bernard Haring's account of the background of Vatican II's discussion on marriage and the family in: "Fostering the Nobility of Marriage and the Family," *Commentary on the Documents of Vatican II*, edited by Herbert Vorgrimler, Vol. V, New York: Herder and Herder, 1969, pp. 225-245.

[32]It is important that a warning be issued concerning a serious mistranslation in the passages concerning marriage from Vatican II. The Abbot translation correctly renders the original Latin in referring to Christian marriage as a covenant. A more recent translation in the edition of the documents from Vatican II by Flannery has the following: "The intimate partnership of life and the love which constitutes the married state has been established by the creator and endowed by him with its own proper laws: it is rooted in the contract of its partners, that is, in their irrevocable personal consent."

[33]Paul Palmer, "Christian Marriage: Contract or Covenant?," pp. 617-619.

justice are still involved.[34] Justice calls forth much of the content of love; they are certainly not opposing virtues. The concerns of sexual equality, which were discussed earlier, are established on a foundation of justice. Granted, love often exceeds the calculations of justice, it must, nevertheless, include the requirements of justice as well.

The covenant model can also be misleading if the biblical covenant between God and his people is uncritically applied to the marital situation.[35] God and humanity are not equals; their covenantal roles are not to be equated. Unlike the divine covenant, the marital relation does not join, *in any sense of the word,* a superior with an inferior.

The exchange of vows expresses a profound mutual commitment of faithful love in the present and for the future. Because much of that future is unknown, including the as yet undiscovered aspects of one's spouse, marital vows are made with no small degree of risk. Many individuals naturally hesitate making this commitment. The vows when pronounced with full knowledge of their intent, involve a change in one's life structure as new priorities are allowed to enter one's life. A me-first philosophy will yield to a we-first pattern if the relationship is to develop the sacramental potential God intends. If their love is authentically Christian each will become for the other a center from which other life values will emanate.[36] From their initial promises will issue new patterns of thinking and behavior which will decidedly challenge the couple, and which will be felt particularly in the early years of marriage.

The mutual consent expressed in the marriage vows, while sufficient for establishing Christian marriage, is augmented by a "sealing" or "completion" in sexual inter-

---

[34]See Tibor Horvath, "Marriage: Contract? Covenant? Community? Sacrament of Sacraments? — Fallible Symbol of Infallible Love, Revelation of Sin and Love," in *The Sacraments: God's Love and Mercy Actualized,* edited by Francis A. Eigo, Villanova: Villanova University Press, 1979, p. 146.

[35]The reference to marriage in the fifth chapter of the Epistle to the Ephesians will be discussed in chapter eight.

[36]Jon Nilson, "The Love at the Center of Love: A Theological Interpretation of Marriage," *Chicago Studies* 18 (1979), p. 243.

course. We already discussed the debate many centuries earlier concerning whether consummation was absolutely necessary for establishing a true Christian marriage.[37] Earlier historical periods valued sexual intercourse particularly because of its procreative significance. Major significance was attributed particularly to the first act of sexual intercourse because it explicitly expressed that meaning.

Today the significance of sex is more clearly related to love in marriage. While not denying the procreative meaning of marital sex, a fuller meaning is now available in the experience of marital sexual love. And if "consummation" is to remain significant in a theological understanding of marriage its meaning should be expanded to encompass not simply "the first time," but to include the pattern of sexual activity throughout marital life.

Sex alone does not define marriage, but marriage can provide a meaning for sex. While sexual activity in marriage is uniquely capable of expressing unconditional marital love, and while most couples remember quite well (for better or worse) their first act of sexual intercourse with each other, sex cannot be identified with the totality of marital life.[38] It is only part of the love which flows between them. Sex, while important, cannot be viewed as totally decisive for defining marriage personally or legalistically, particularly within a Christian framework.

Marital sex is capable of expressing a broad range of values and meaning. Sometimes it hardly honors the dignity of marriage. This is becoming more known as instances of marital "rape" are being reported. Yet, its potential for enriching the marital relationship remains. Rosemary Haughton suggests that in the fifth chapter of Ephesians, with a comparison noted between Christ's relation to the church and the marriage relationship, we find that both unions involve a sharing of bodies.[39] Paul's theology of

[37]For a fine summary of this debate see Andre Guindon, "Case for a 'Consummated' Sexual Bond before a 'Ratified' Marriage," *Eglise et Theologie* 8(1977), pp. 137-181.

[38]See Dwight Harvey Small, *Christian: Celebrate Your Sexuality*, pp. 180-183.

[39]Rosemary Haughton, *The Passionate God*, p. 222.

Christ's body being given for all also has significant implications for married Christians. In sharing bodies, life itself is exchanged.

Marriage celebrated in the midst of the church community can also become a unique moment in the faith life of the couple. John Paul II describes the exchange of vows as "the basic moment of the faith of the couple."[40] Ascribing such significance flows from the kind of interpersonal commitment Christian marriage demands. Christian faith in forming marriage ought not to be viewed as additional to the interpersonal event, like frosting on the cake. Rather, it is effectively operative within that act through which people vow unconditional love for another person. A church wedding makes explicit this faith dimension. It brings the joining of the human with the divine into the open first for the couple, and then for the community.

Today a serious pastoral concern exists within the church over allowing people to ritualize their marriage within the church when there appear few indications, if any, that the couple is actively living a Christian faith. Sometimes the man and/or woman are referred to as baptized non-Christians. This often happens when a person is baptized as an infant, and thereafter sees little of the inside of a church until requesting permission to "use" the church for one's wedding. The question becomes whether a church wedding would misrepresent the nature of the church and the values it stands for as well as the meaning of Christian marriage.

This issue is further complicated by the difficulty of formulating clear criteria for determining who is a genuine Christian. Regular participation in the liturgy of the local church, while one sign of a living faith, cannot be viewed as the only standard for faith because in some ways that custom can be culturally conditioned. There are instances where the males in a given community are simply unaccustomed to going to church, and while this may indicate an imperfect faith, it may be explained more as a symptom of a distorted culture.

[40]John Paul II, "On the Family," Section 51.

At the International Synod of Bishops in Rome in 1980, the issue was placed before John Paul II. It was described in terms of special pastoral urgency, particularly in traditional Catholic cultures which had undergone widespread secular erosion in recent years. With Matrimony understood as a sacrament of living faith, concerned pastors sought guidance in those cases where the Christian faith appeared quite dormant in couples approaching the church for marriage.

It might be noted, in passing, that one of the reasons why marriage was not thought to be a sacrament of grace in the early Middle Ages was due to its need for a great degree of faith. So much depended, it was thought, on the spiritual maturity of the couple. It shared that "problem" with the rite of reconciliation or penance. So much seemed to depend on the attitude or dispositions of the recipients of these sacraments. A way around that historical issue was found as the conviction developed within the church that married couples really *needed* God's help or grace to overcome the many difficulties of married life, and to "purify" the sexual side of marriage. Therefore, it eventually was concluded that grace was offered to the couple, provided they did not block its reception.

It seems that a similar type of thinking was also behind John Paul's response to the concerns of the 1980 Synod. While noting that the engaged often lack perfection in faith and seek a church wedding for more social than religious reasons, the Pope advocated pastoral sensitivity and receptivity. God's generosity is abundant. If only a shred of evidence indicates openness on the part of the couple, the church community should grasp that and welcome the couple into its presence. John Paul II argues the case in the following way:

> "Nevertheless, it must not be forgotten that these engaged couples by virtue of their baptism are already really sharers in Christ's marriage covenant with the church, and that, by their right intention, they have accepted God's plan regarding marriage and therefore at

least implicitly consent to what the church intends to do when she celebrates marriage. Thus the fact that motives of a social nature also enter into the request is not enough to justify refusal on the part of pastors. Moreover, as the Second Vatican Council teaches, the sacraments by words and ritual elements nourish and strengthen faith: that faith toward which the married couple are already journeying by reason of the uprightness of their intention, which Christ's grace certainly does not fail to favor and support."[41]

While a rather broad pastoral approach may be taken to the existential faith of the couple requesting marriage in the church, there remains a critical need to prepare couples for sacramental marriage as much as this is possible in each concrete case. Just like the other sacraments of the church, Matrimony is not a magical activity which automatically enriches faith life or personal growth. It will be life-giving to the degree that the individual couple is responsibly open to, understands, and cooperates with God's movement in their life. God does not force individuals against their freedom. This principle of active cooperation with God applies, of course, to all human activity. But it is particularly applicable to the Christian sacraments since they are each related to God's presence and power at significant moments of life.

Preparation for Christian marriage ought to include two basic areas of learning. First, an intensification of one's knowledge of the person one intends to marry. Love is rooted in knowledge, and for love to be genuine, healthy and realistic, it must be founded on a totally open-eyed awareness of the beloved. Interpersonal marital love certainly involves a lifelong process. But the more love is rooted in truth before marriage, the more one's marital vows will be genuine expressions of personal affirmation based on reality and better foundation on which to build upon in the years ahead.

Second, since Christian marriage includes serious implications for one's faith life, preparation ought to include

[41] *Ibid.*

processes which ready one for full reception of God within marriage. A correspondence exists between the deepening of one's relationship with God, and the enrichment of interpersonal life. While it may be appropriate to distinguish interpersonal and spiritual preparation for Christian marriage, fundamentally the issue is the same: opening oneself to receive personal mystery into one's life. In the words of a Christian hymn: Wherever charity and love prevail, there God is ever found.

A basis for calling marriage a sacrament was once sought by "proving" that Jesus instituted the sacrament of Matrimony at the wedding feast at Cana. Today such an approach is unacceptable because the evidence sought was simply not there in the biblical story. Yet approaching the Cana event for different reasons may yield fresh insight into the role of wedding feasts in the life of the Kingdom. More than any other type of gathering in New Testament times, the wedding feast was an exuberant and lavish celebration of love. Today's biblical research notes that the amorous and even erotic verses of the Song of Songs originated and were at home in that setting. With the arrival of the Kingdom Jesus proclaimed that, more than anything else, it was a community of love. How appropriate it was, therefore, for the Lord to manifest for the first time an explicit sign of the Kingdom in the midst of a wedding banquet. Not only was Jesus present for the festivities, he kept the party going!

Many factors can deplete the richness of a Christian wedding. Too much concern over legal considerations, an encrustation which sometimes occurs when the meaning of rituals have been forgotten, anxiety over propriety and performance, and the stifling of the spirit caused by overconcern for appearances, all work to weaken the power which is potentially available in the celebration of today's wedding feast. Good celebration, of course, arises much more from the personal qualities of the celebrators than from any material elements used in the festivities.

From the spiritual standpoint the celebration is viewed in the church as a moment of special grace with its high point being the exchange of marital vows. God is always present to people, but there are certain times when the people are more present to God. And these are often moments of deep interpersonal awareness. In protecting and valuing the rituals of Matrimony, the church desires to alert both those marrying and the community which witnesses their marriage that this time is sacred. It is important in itself, and therefore deserves to be celebrated for its own sake. It is also important because it is the first step in what will hopefully be a long journey for the couple as they begin to share their life journey with each other.

The celebration of Christian marriage through formal sacramental rites does not exhaust the meaning of the sacrament. It is a stage in the enactment of the sacrament.[42] Its meaning accompanies them as they leave the church to enter marital life. A developmental view of Matrimony is absolutely necessary if, as Vatican II taught, the sacrament of marriage is appreciated as a community of life and love. John Paul II captures this dimension of marriage in well-chosen words: "God who called the couple to marriage, continues to call them in marriage."[43] Our next consideration must be, therefore, an account of Christian marriage as a journey down, what could be, a very long, trying, and exciting road.

[42]James M. Schmeiser, "Marriage in Contemporary Society," p. 108.
[43]John Paul II, "On the Family," Section 51.

CHAPTER V:
SEASONED THROUGH CHANGE

In 1946 a Public Affairs pamphlet dealing with the topic of marriage began with the following statement:

> "Getting married is really little more than the signing of a contract to build a marriage. It is a required first step. But it does not build the marriage any more than an engineer's contract automatically builds a bridge. The real building is done later over a period of time, through the application of a great deal of skill and energy. So it is with marriage. A marriage that is strong enough to stand the strains and stresses of modern living requires the cooperative efforts of the two contractors through the years."[1]

Almost half a century later this point rings even more true. A great deal of social change has taken place in the intervening decades, with much of it having a direct bearing on the all so fragile relationship between wife and husband.

[1]Evelyn Millis Duvall, *Building Your Marriage*, New York: Public Affairs Pamphlets, 1946, p. 1.

111

Like the retention of freedom, maintaining a marriage today requires constant vigilance and determined effort. Societal norms now view divorce as a reasonable, acceptable solution to marital problems. Families rarely, if ever, ostracize divorced members. We live in a climate of tolerance which, it can be added, is clearly an advance over one which emphasized condemnation as a primary form of social control. Nevertheless, as has been noted earlier in the book, if a marriage is to survive, its strength and vitality will largely have to come from the convictions and values personally held by the couple. Their religious beliefs can have a decided impact on how their marriage continues.

In the last chapter we discussed the factors which contribute to, or detract from, a church wedding. Swiss theologian, Karl Barth has commented that the Catholic Church has traditionally been more interested in the wedding than in the ensuing marriage. Identifying the marriage with the wedding was, for Barth, "a dreaded and deep-rooted error."[2] He accepted the value of recognizing the married status of the couple at the time of the wedding. But, he added that the *religious* dimension of marriage was more properly attributed to married life which only began with the wedding. We should examine some of the reasons why the church traditionally maintained this misplaced emphasis.

The church crystallized much of its understanding of the sacraments during the thirteenth century with the aid of the intellectual ferment which swept through the newly-formed universities and schools. It was a time when tired theological concepts, inherited from the Dark Ages, were reformulated in relation to the best of philosophical and scientific thought of the era. As we saw in the last chapter, the theology of marriage formulated at the conclusion of the thirteenth century was left mostly intact until the developments introduced by Vatican II.

---

[2]Karl Barth, *Church Dogmatics*, III/4, Edinburgh: T. and T. Clark, 1961, p. 225. For an analysis of Barth's theology of marriage, see David M. Thomas, *Karl Barth's Theology of Marriage*, Ann Arbor: University Microfilms, 1971.

While past gains, particularly in the works of St. Thomas Aquinas, injected vitality into religious thought, this dynamism was soon snuffed out by a legalism which filled the churches in the following centuries. Sacramental doctrines were translated into prescriptions of law. Often a minimalist approach was taken in describing the sacraments, focusing only on the proper enactment of the rite for validity. With respect to the sacrament of marriage, it was generally considered enough that the couple married according to the proper ceremonial form. What happened after the wedding day was the sole concern of the couple.

Another reason for this rather narrow approach to the sacraments was the existence of a society which knew little of social mobility. This explains, in part, why the sacramental theology of the past appears so lifeless in contrast to today's more personalistic and developmental approach. Prior to the sixteenth century life was almost entirely determined by one's family of origin. Travel was limited unless one was sent away to war. Class distinctions were fixed. Marriage was often based on a decision made more by one's family than by the couple directly involved. While not totally unknown before the modern era, marriage was rarely spoken of in terms of love. And romantic love, a love distinguished by heterosexual excitement and interest, was almost always defined as nonmarital in nature.

In official church teaching, new ground was gradually opened up starting with Pope Pius XI in his encyclical letter on marriage released on the last day of the year 1930. I will quote at length from this document because it was one of the first major attempts on the part of the church to deal with married life and love as it unfolded after the wedding. In his discussion of married love the Pope offered the following reflections:

> "The love, then, of which we are speaking is not that based on the passing lust of the moment nor does it consist in pleasing words only, but in the deep attachment of the heart which is expressed in action, since love is proved by deeds. This outward expression of love in the

home demands not only mutual help but must go further; it must have as its primary purpose that man and wife help each other day by day in forming and perfecting themselves in the interior life, so that through their partnership in life they may advance ever more and more in virtue, and above all that they may grow in true love toward God and their neighbour, on which indeed "dependeth the whole Law and Prophets" (Mt. 22:40). For all men of every condition, in whatever honorable walk of life they may be, can and ought to imitate the most perfect example of holiness placed before man by God, namely Christ Our Lord, and by God's grace to arrive at the summit of perfection, as is proved by the example set us of many saints.

This mutual inward moulding of husband and wife; this determined effort to perfect each other, can in a very real sense, as the Roman Catechism teaches, be said to be the chief reason and purpose of matrimony, provided matrimony be looked at not in the restricted sense as instituted for the proper conception and education of the child, but more widely as the blending of life as a whole and the mutual interchange and sharing thereof."[3]

What begins to be noticed, as exemplified in this document by Pius XI, is that the twentieth century presents a world of accelerated change. Every major discipline incorporates in some way dynamic models or frameworks to describe the real world. Currently, this trend has expanded to include interest in mapping developmental stages throughout life, particularly during the adult years. For example, the seminal work of Daniel Levinson and his associates suggests alternating phases of transition and stability occurring regularly throughout adult life, spanning periods or seasons of approximately ten years at length.[4] Research is progressing to determine whether male and

[3]Pius XI, "On Christian Marriage," in *Love and Sexuality, Official Catholic Teachings*, Wilmington: McGrath Publishing Co., sections 49 and 50.

[4]Daniel Levinson *et al., The Seasons of a Man's Life*, New York: Ballantine Books, 1978.

female patterns are similar. Initial results appear to indicate that while the content and scheduling of the seasons may differ somewhat, there remains a pattern of reoccurring stasis and movement for both men and women.

How is this research of interest to religious thought? How might it affect our thinking about Christian marriage? Theology today affirms connections or an interrelationship between human and divine meaning. Therefore, these "discoveries" of change-patterns in human life deserve serious consideration by anyone attempting to map God's involvement in creation. They invite a new awareness of time and its meaning for the Christian life. In the language of Vatican II, "the signs of the times" might be read with greater clarity in both personal and marital life if the promising insights are taken seriously while also taking proper steps to insure their truthfulness.

In general, research in the stages of adult life have focused upon the individual subject. What is needed in a reflection on marriage is a mapping of relational change which highlights the patterns common to the beginning the middle, and the mature seasons of a marriage. And this is being done, although it would have to be noted that such descriptions must be taken with an open mind since they are based on relatively few studies.

Particular research has been centered on the first decade of marriage. This is probably due to the fact that change during these years is more apparent and lays a foundation for all that follows. The natural processes of adjustment are intensively operative in the first years of marriage.

Based on research done at the National Opinion Research Center, a rough profile of these years has been sketched. A report of the research describes a pattern involving four stages: 1) falling in love, 2) settling-down, 3) bottoming-out, and 4) beginning again.[5] These patterns may be understood as not only having secular meaning, but also, a deeper meaning might be interpreted because these changes in

[5]Joan Meyer Anzia and Mary G. Durkin, *Marital Intimacy: A Catholic Perspective*, Kansas City: Andrews and McMeel, Inc., 1980.

marriage bear a remarkable likeness to changes in personal religious life.[6] These findings suggest that the dynamics of relational life, whether it be one's relationship to God or to a human being, parallel each other, and even more to the point, influence each other. It would indicate another way of saying that the love of God and the love of neighbor cannot be separated.

Any significant relational event occurring within marriage must be considered part of marriage viewed as a sacrament. It is myopic to view Matrimony as related only to the wedding; it must be related to the total dynamics of the marriage. The challenges of marital life, the good days and the not so good, all contribute to the content of sacramental life in marriage. This adds realism to the theology and challenge to the couple. In Hannah Green's *I Never Promised You a Rose Garden*, she argues that most essential to adult love is the element of challenge. While a world of perfect order and bliss may exist in the mind of the lover, in the end, such a world can only be a deception, a lie, and will become, if pursued in itself, a bore as well.[7]

This chapter will explore the issue of sacramental married life from three perspectives. *First*, I will present a Christian understanding of time. God gives us time to use for transforming creation into the Kingdom. Each Christian marriage is a love unit within the Kingdom. Time is the opportunity given for us to love. Mining the treasure of each day requires a special alertness to what's expected by God. *Second*, with Christian marriage designed by God to create lifelong intimacy, I will examine marital intimacy as it is related to seasons within marriage. The value of romantic love in marriage has recently received interesting support from a variety of disciplines.

Romantic love, however, remains somewhat problematic because of the many meanings it has. Possessing a clear

---

[6]Andrew M. Greeley, *The Young Catholic Famiy: Religious Images and Marital Fulfillment*, Chicago: The Thomas More Press, 1980.

[7]Hannah Green, *I Never Promised You a Rose Garden*, New York: Signet Books, 1964, p. 106.

sense of its positive potential in adult love can help couples even into the autumn years of marriage.

Third, while marriage may have many features which, more or less, come naturally to a couple, there remain skills which can be learned to enhance the love life of a couple. Most of the "how-to" books relating to marriage are simply guidebooks for developing useful skills which promote honest and healthy love relationships. Would that these skills were regularly taught in all families as children were nurtured. Unfortunately, too few families promote or practice good techniques in communication, conflict-resolution, or awareness. Yet, many of these skills can be learned during adult life. Anyone claiming no need whatsoever for personal improvement in relational skills is probably most in need.

For marriage to last, one of the most practical skills is that of forgiveness. While rooted often in deep religious conviction, it too has elements which can be learned. In a sense, marriage provides its participants one of the most important settings for learning how to live the gift of life most completely.

A Christian Reflection on Time

To love someone is to give that person your time. And in that time there can develop an ever deeper loving relationship. There can also occur what most would call one of life's greatest tragedies, the death of love. In itself, time is like a blank page. It can be filled with meaning if we humans invest in the opportunities provided by the "space" of time. If we give nothing time is wasted; but time is rendered precious if we give much. The greatest gift anyone can give is their life for another person. Christianity is built on this principle.

Scripture is filled with references to time. In the beginning God created. In the fullness of time Christ came. At the end of time the Lord will again return. God takes time very seriously. The value of time is determined not only by the hands of a clock but by the opportunities it provides.

Applied to marriage, the time available after the wedding is a series of opportunities which can be filled with marital love. This time can be wasted, or it can issue forth in relational richness. Neither outcome arises spontaneously. It all depends on the openness, the awareness, the caring, and the commitment of the couple involved.

Recent theological reflection likes to emphasize the freedom available in every human event. God endows each person with the gift of freedom. While limitations of all kinds impinge upon virtually every human act, for instance, all people are at least partially victimized by their personal history, there must remain a zone of free choice, protected and valued so that personal acts and decisions are truly one's own. Some desire to flee personal responsibility by not accepting the burden of freedom. This temptation inflicts most from time to time. People are often very adept at formulating excuses or reasons which rule out personal responsibility. I am not referring here to moments of compulsiveness, but to freely chosen personal orientations which are designed to exempt one from personal responsibility. Given our cultural emphasis on the passivity of the experience of love, as evidenced by phrases like "falling in love" or "being in love," the temptation to escape from responsibility even there is all the more real.

Marriage can fail as we all know. As in other matters, many excuses are given for its demise. People can be very imaginative in creating stories as to how "it happened." Some may say, "It just didn't work out." Others may conclude that "it just wasn't in the cards." Some of these explanations are useful in that they allow people to continue on after failure with personal integrity still intact. This should not be put down. Yet most who fail, if honest with themselves and the routes taken during the marriage, will confess to a failure in using the opportunities offered within marriage for enrichment of the relationship. It is also important that the church, with its central belief in God's merciful forgiveness, be present to those who have failed.

These reflections on freedom and responsibility are important to establish a simple, yet significant point for the married: God expects much from each Christian marriage, and will never hold back any needed help, but it will depend on the generosity of the couples themselves to accomplish this task.

I have consciously avoided using the word "development" in relation to marriage. It is not that I am personally against marital growth, but I have witnessed too many examples where the concept of development has confused or even destroyed people — and without reason. We live in a culture so effected by the human potential movement, along with the pop psychology it has generated, that people become victims of many partial truths. If they are unable to understand the meaning of reasonable growth through the challenges and changes offered by life, they often demand too much and end up being disheartened by the results.

While there may be many more reasons for avoiding developmental concepts, I note here ten which make me hesitant to use them. 1) Developmental language victimizes individuals who possess perfectionistic tendencies and leaves them without defence against unrealistic goals they impulsively formulate. 2) In developmental models for marriage, growth is expected for both spouses which often causes one spouse to be highly critical of the other's "growth" (or lack of it). 3) Developmental models tend to emphasize goals, but pay little attention to the means needed to attain such goals. Concern is more for tomorrow than for today. This can be escapist and draw attention away from where it should be placed: on the moment at hand. 4) To acquire the satisfaction of success, proof is required. Yet given the complexity of the marriage relationship, no single test is able to determine adequately successful development. Individual proofs can give a distorted or misleading assessment of a marriage. 5) The value given to developing a successful career, earning large sums of money or material possessions, in today's society can lead one to equate success in these areas with success in marriage. While it is possible to achieve success in many areas of life, success in one doesn't insure success in the others. 6) If the goal sought is defined as marital unity, the couple might create this unity by absorption, that is, one person's life being dissolved into the other's. This may cause a joining of two by becoming one, but in a sense which hardly dignifies Christian marriage. Total oneness might be brought about as one person denies himself or herself with this being understood almost literally. 7) Success in both a personalistic and religious sense is often paradoxical. What on one level appears as loss can actually be gain. Christianity itself is built on this principle. 8) Some models of development are so fixed on radical change that any sense of personal or historical continuity is overlooked. While many couples will be able to locate "turning points" in their relationship, there will always be a "carry over" from before they gained new insight and status in their relationship. 9) The desire to develop might be quite self-centered. While it is certainly not necessary that "progress" for the two be identical, some sense of the needs and rights of the spouse must always be a part of marital life. Marriage is not a solo-trip of two. 10) Concern for development can miss the need to accept each person "as he or she is." Granted each person should desire what is best for the other (and it should be the "best" for the other, not *my* view of what's best), there remains the value of radical acceptance, a love that is concretely for the spouse right now.[8]

I have stated my concern for models of development because they are often bought without criticism or even awareness of the many ways developmental models can be a disservice to healthy marital life. I support, however, the need to use the many opportunities provided by the time of marriage for deepening the marital relationship. But just as traditional descriptions of spiritual development note "dark nights" or periods of spiritual aridity when no progress appears evident (yet, in reality, significant growth could be taking place), I contend that something similar happens in marriage. During the dry spells, the individual may be required to proceed more by simple will power than by the emotional satisfaction. If God works one way along the

[8]See Anzia and Durkin, *Marital Intimacy*, p. 38.

journey to spiritual perfection, is it not reasonable to assume that the same dynamics are in effect in Christian marriage. We should not expect the patterns of the divine-human relationship to differ essentially from those which operate within the God-given challenges of marital life. Both are present in relationships of interpersonal intimacy.

In the spiritual life, the periods of dryness serve to purify the individual of self-centeredness. God desires a genuine relationship of mutuality, and not one based simply on the enjoyment which God may provide. The early stages of the spiritual life are often described in terms of emotional satisfaction, particularly during the experience of prayer. Friendship, in general, and marriage, in particular, follow a similar pattern. Young love is filled with the highs of personal enjoyment. Sometimes almost ecstatic pleasure comes from just thinking about the beloved. But as the days pass some of that feeling wanes and one is tempted to wonder whether true love is drifting away. Many popular songs and poems are composed with this question in mind.

Yet, rather than indicating love's departure, a change in feeling may introduce a transformation where one's attention and interest become more altruistic. In marriage desire for personal feelings drawn from the spouse are replaced by desires to please the spouse. A me-centered world is changed into a we-centered world.

In marriage deep, honest, and intensive love can be set in motion.[9] Through a process of purification genuine love is given the opportunity to unfold, purged of the destructive element of self-centeredness. The Kingdom of love is allowed to be more real. Just as the crowds became smaller when Jesus notified his listeners that the Kingdom would include the cross, so Christian marriage may appear, to those who grasp its demands, somewhat frightening. And because of its demands for mature and honest love, Christian marriage qualifies as an important setting for sanctity to occur. Part of the demands include a willingness to use

[9]Daniel Day Williams, *The Spirit and Forms of Love*, p. 138.

the various crises of relational life which occur rather regularly when people live in the kind of closeness demanded by the intimate sharing of marital life and love — which, by the way, is the definition given to Christian marriage by Vatican II.

If marital growth (understood, of course, correctly) is required by the sacramental nature of marriage, it is important to sketch some of the ways the married might fail to meet this goal. An understanding of the negative side of marital life puts into sharper relief its positive side.

First, it should be noted that sins against marriage are best identified as sins against love. While this can be said about all sinfulness, mention of this here has particular value because sin is often linked with a sense of defilement especially when sex is part of the discussion. Moral treatises about marriage traditionally focused too narrowly on sexual issues. They failed to take into account the general relational tenor of the marriage.

One way of understanding sin is that it blocks the love of God which God intended to be a part of human and personal history. We are instruments through which God's life-giving love comes into the world. God can be frustrated, so to speak, by our failure to use opportunities to love through concrete care and service. God's gracious power is rendered inept and the power of evil, the power of nothingness, is allowed to prevail.[10]

Traditional theology distinguishes between sins of commission (moral evil caused) and sins of omission (moral good which was left undone). Personal growth in moral rectitude usually involves a passage from avoiding the evil toward the doing of the good. As moral sensitivity deepens, the individual becomes more aware of opportunities to do that which is better and more creative of a world filled with love.[11]

---

[10]See Rosemary Haughton, *The Passionate God*, pp. 112-113.

[11]An excellent survey of recent developments in moral theology is found in Timothy E. O'Connell, *Principles for a Catholic Morality,* New York: The Seabury Press, 1979.

For married Christians, the pursuit of virtue will certainly involve refraining from acts of hurtfulness. But it should also involve a positive pursuit of the good, of extending oneself in favor of one's wife or husband. Morality and spirituality should blend. The avoidance of deceit will evolve into a habit of telling the truth in all matters. Forms of spousal abuse will be replaced by tenderness and sensitivity. Instead of considering the obligation of fidelity a burden, it will be viewed as a privilege as one freely chooses one's spouse as the single most important person in one's life.

While a catalogue of marital vices and virtues may appear rather mundane, nevertheless, it is out of the mundane, daily interaction of wife and husband that a healthy and holy Christian marriage is formed. It requires effort and an overcoming of those natural defenses which we all erect to keep people at a distance. As a marriage unfolds it is right and proper that defenses be dismantled so that intimacy may increase.

While this may be desired, the testimony of professional marriage counselors indicates that in early years of marriage there occurs an interesting, and sometimes tragic, phenomenon. It goes something like this. Most marry with the intention of being honest in all matters. Accompanying the willingness to be candid and forthright is a sometimes naive belief that on most matters the newlyweds agree. It does not take long for an event or experience to occur which jars the couple by revealing some point of significant difference between them. It scares many because they begin to wonder whether there are other areas of difference, which may be hidden because they simply haven't been discussed. To protect the marriage from further "discord," the couple may decide to refrain from any topic of conversation which might cause argument or disagreement. The continuing revelation of each person is therefore blocked by the fear of discovering something in the other or of exposing something in the self which may not be a delight. An element of risk will be a part of all future conversations. Each person will have to grow in acceptance and tolerance should the process of mutual self-revelation continue. The meaning of truthfulness in marriage will take on new significance.

It takes time to make a good Christian marriage. Its growth cannot be left to natural causes because if left to its own, the marriage will atrophy and die. It must be fed by honest communication and caring acts of love and sensitivity. That is what time is for in God's loving plan: it provides an opportunity to fill its emptiness with the love God desires to be expressed and felt as the face of the earth is renewed.

The Seasons of Marital Intimacy

I prefer the concept of season to that of developmental growth because it emphasizes that there is an appropriateness to each stage of marital life. In other words, it is healthy and virtuous for young marrieds to be somewhat self-centered and immature. Their love for each other will be flavored with a touch of illusion. In due time their awareness of each other will be purified and made more truthful.

The concept of romantic love is usually applied to love in its early stages. Recent literature in psychology has made an important distinction with regard to types of romantic love.[12] On the one hand, there is a romantic love that is quite passive in nature and almost compulsive in its operation. It more or less happens to one, thus creating the language of "falling in love." Little can be done to initiate its beginning or prevent its demise. It is no wonder that it is often considered under the control of blind fate or some other form of supernatural force. Some may term it infatuation or puppy love, yet its effect on its "victims" is often startling and serious — while it lasts. Those under the influence of this type of attraction are convinced that life will no longer be worth living should love die. It is filled with a dreamlike

[12]See Nathaniel Branden, *The Psychology of Romantic Love*, Los Angeles: J. P. Tarcher, Inc., 1980.

quality and is quite prone to idealizing the beloved. This kind of love is responsible for the phrase "love is blind." Making serious decisions while under the influence of this type of romantic love can be dangerous and foolhardy.

It can have positive value as well. In many cases it awakens the individual to new and exciting aspects of personal life. It alerts one to other people in a way never before experienced. It can trigger a social sense dormant until the moment that special someone entered one's life. Usually, or almost inevitably, this love tends to burn with a short fuse and either dies a rather quick death or is transformed into a love which is more altruistic and open-eyed.

But does this mean that the feelings and excitement of romantic love are forever lost? Can only the young enjoy its benefits? Not at all. The initial phases of romantic love occur largely outside the realm of conscious choice, and to further its possibilities in more mature form entails a more active role by those who would desire its benefits, and a significant decision to live out the deeper, more lasting implications of all that was sensed in the Springtime of its life.[13]

The blindness of its early phase is supplanted by clearer vision. In fact, that which is seen by the one who loves can be the deepest truth about the other person in that the lover will look harder and longer to discover the full richness of the beloved. Each will want to know more so that more can be loved and cherished.[14] Mature love will also allow for a greater degree of self-revelation. Possessing a sense that one is fundamentally loved for all that one is allows a lowering of defenses. This is never easy but it can be done if it is felt to be desirable and if one senses that even warts and wrinkles will be cherished.[15]

The passage from immature to mature love is not instantaneous. It is part of that long journey walked by the couple.

[13]Haughton, *The Passionate God*, p. 91.

[14]Branden, *The Psychology of Romantic Love,* p. 145.

[15]*Ibid.*, p. 83.

There will be many crises each of which contains an opportunity for deepening the marital relationship.[16] Adjustments of idealizations or projections, to borrow the language of C. G. Jung, will happen as life together unfolds. Many of these reorientations will be painful; others may cause great delight. It is all part of the journey through uncharted territory. After all, each married couple is in for discoveries never before witnessed or experienced in history. What I find in my wife, what she discovers in me, what we each learn about ourselves because of that which is drawn to the surface by the other, is all new. From a sacramental perspective, something about God is also brought to light in this most sacred process of interpersonal revelation.

Adjustments of personal priorities, the use of time and money, modifications of hobbies, leisure pursuits and lifestyle may all, at one time or another, come under the type of thinking required to change a private journey into one that is more shared. This prospect need not be viewed, however, as inimical. Is not one of the primary reasons for marrying in the first place, the desire to live with another person, to expand one's experience of life through a joining with another? The sharing of many sunrises and sunsets can add significant beauty to the colors perceived in viewing these events. It is an old and true adage that joys shared are doubled as sorrows shared are halved when experienced with one you love.

Realism requires an adjustment process which includes positive ways of dealing with disagreeable aspects of each other, and the working toward overcoming the inevitable conflicts which occur when two people of different background and sex, attempt to walk side-by-side through life. Call this process conflict-resolution, negotiation, haggling, or simply deciding what color to paint the kitchen and you have an aspect of marriage which is central for survival. Each couple will work this out in their own way. Usually, a private discussion and resolution will occur between the

[16]See Evelyn Eaton Whitehead and James D. Whitehead, *Marrying Well: Possibilities of Christian Marriage Today*, Garden City: Doubleday, 1981, pp. 97 - 179.

wife and husband. In extreme circumstances, when the domestic setting fails, the conversation may involve the services of a friend, a clergyperson, or a professional counselor. Fortunately, the skills of a trained "arbitrator" are available to most couples, and the use of professional help in solving marital problems is no longer viewed in terms of failure. It is even argued that couples might meet with a professional counselor in much the same way they would arrange for regular physical check-ups with a physician. What this indicates, perhaps, is a growing consensus that all marriages need help from time to time, with successful marriages being among those who courageously use it.

Forming a Christian conjugal community involves a special kind of openness and acceptance. It also involves mutual respect. The word "respect" is formed from the combination of two Latin words which joined mean literally, "to look again." Respect implies going beyond the surface to perceive the deeper beauty hidden to the passerby. From a respectful attitude comes the truth each person embodies, a truth unique which relates to part of the reason God created one as a special reflection of God's identity. The lifetime of a marriage is an on-going opportunity to draw into creation some never-before-revealed facet of God's beauty. If the opportunity is missed the Kingdom will be less than it might have been. While this process applies in every instance of human exchange, in marriage it has a special meaning because of the depth of mutuality possible in the on-going encounter of wife and husband.

This process involves unfolding part of the mystery of God through spousal exchange of two living, dynamic persons. Again, the awareness of the many stages of adult "passages" is part of the roadsigns which guide the couple in directing their journey. Individual changes occur which prompt each partner to let the other in on one's movement whether it be psychological, intellectual, physical, or spiritual — or all of these together. In Lillian Hellman's play *Toys in the Attic* one of the characters notes sadly how this type of communication can be overlooked with tragic results. One of her characters is overheard saying, "Well, people change and forget to tell each other. Too bad — causes so many mistakes."[17]

While the word intimacy is often ambiguous in meaning because it is applied to even superficial exchanges, when used correctly the concept points to a process central to marital life. Each person has levels of significance which are only gradually exposed to the view of another, like peeling back the layers of an onion. Normally mutual understanding will begin with the intellectual — a sharing of perceptions, experiences, and how one thinks about various events or persons outside oneself. As affection develops physical exchanges occur which communicate something deeper, more hidden in each person. Finally the inner-self is revealed: one's emotional and spiritual treasures are shared.[18] The process of mutual exchange can occur quite slowly or it can be stimulated to move more quickly. It is important to remember the fact that unless the interchange is done in freedom and with respect for the integrity of each other's personal style of revealing the end result will not bring greater intimacy, but alienation.

The road toward intimacy is perhaps the most arduous of the marital journey. Many choose a safer route involving communication largely on "safe" topics, mostly extrinsic to the interpersonal relation of wife and husband. To face each other in full honesty is never easy. Deep in many is a fear that if one were really known rejection or ridicule might follow. Maybe people are born with a certain degree of spontaneous freedom in self-expression, but today's culture seems to root this out and replace it with caution. There may be reasons for this, but good arguments can also be marshalled for relearning the art of free personal expression. In the lifetime of a marriage there will be many chances for enriching conversation between wife and husband. As mutual knowledge deepens, greater love can blossom. The

[17] As quoted in Robert Lee and Majorie Casebier, *The Spouse Gap: Weathering the Marriage Crisis During Middlescence,* Nashville: Abingdon Press, 1971, p. 14.

[18] See Alan M. Dahms, "Intimacy Hierarchy," in *Process in Relationship,* edited by Edward A. Powers and Mary Lees, St. Paul: West Publishing Co., 1974, pp. 73-92.

acquisition of relational skills in contemporary marriage is not a luxury, it provides the fuel for keeping the journey moving.

Enrichment Skills for Lasting Marriages

We began this chapter by quoting from a pamphlet about marriage written soon after World War II. In that same publication, which may seem almost archaic in literature dealing with modern marriage, we find this timeless piece of advice: "Sturdy loves like sturdy plants must be fed and cared for if they are to remain healthy."[19] And if the pressures working against longevity in marriage were great at that time, how might we evaluate their influence today? Already noted is the fact that at best our society is indifferent to the survival of marital unions. Further, a case can be made that because of longer lifespans, more mobility in contemporary life, high expectations for sexual fulfillment, and a general lifestyle that often limits the time spouses have for each other, any marriage which survives deserves special accolades. In some states the number of marriages and divorces are almost equal in number. In some counties, there are even more divorces than marriages recorded each year.

Taking a passive attitude toward the survival of one's marriage is equivalent to jumping out of an airplane at 10,000 feet without a parachute. Since Christian belief holds that marriage is intended by God to last "until death," it is incumbent for couples to develop attitudes necessary for the long journey while developing skills useful for that kind of trek. And it is not simply the time factor which is central. More important is what might be termed the journey to the center of each other's person where intimate life can be shared.

Developing a realistic strategy for relational enrichment begins with some basic principles from time-management.

[19]Duvall, *Building Your Marriage*, p. 7.

Space during the day or the week can be scheduled for the couple to be together without distractions or interruptions. As obvious as this may appear, many neglect this need, particularly when there are other important demands on time. As one marriage counselor put it, "Much more important than *what* you do is *that* you do something and do it regularly."[20] In making a promise before each other and God that "until death do us part," one also promises that in life "we do join." We noted in an earlier chapter that marital love must be concrete and communicated. It will fail in this regard if the couple does not use opportunities for enriching each other in honest communication and expressions of caring.

One of the so-called predictors of marital success is the number of shared-interests possessed by the couple prior to their marriage. If they share an interest in certain types of music, athletics, food, etc., their chances of success are greater. But what about interests which might be developed after the wedding? We do not have to be reminded that adults can learn new skills and develop new interests all through the lifespan. Applied to marriage, it would appear that couples ought, regularly and consciously, to seek new areas of common interest which are developed as a *product* of the marriage. While this may not be judged on the surface as a religious aspect of marriage, it is because it is intended to enrich that "in-between" sacred space between the wife and husband, that special space where their lives touch and God is always present.

The importance of honest marital communication is difficult to overemphasize. Communication, however, should not be viewed as an end in itself, but rather as a means through which love can expand. Much attention has been given to the emotional aspects of interpersonal communication — the feelings, both positive or negative, it generates, the freeing effect of expressing pent-up affection or hostility. While these features are part of healthy interchange, the

[20]Edward Ford, *Permanent Love: Practical Steps to a Lasting Relationship*, Minneapolis: Winston Press, Inc., 1979., p. 39.

accent must also be placed on what can result from the exchange: outcomes such as a new awareness or understanding of each other, a resolution to improve personal behavior, a deepened conviction concerning the worth of the spouse, or a decision to work more effectively for the marriage.[21] It should also be remembered that conversation without genuine love can be no more than an act of manipulation, where the intent might simply be to shape the marriage partner into one's own image and likeness.

Communication is also a means of working through marital conflict. Recall the answer to the question, "how do porcupines make love?" They do it "very carefully," of course. The same can be said for us. As we grow closer together, we notice more clearly the differences which exist between each of us. And differences often breed conflict. In fact, one of the sure signs that the intimacy barrier has been crossed is the feeling that some conflict exists, even between those who love each other. The experience of conflict in marriage need not be interpreted negatively. Conflicts are problematic only when they are ignored or passed over as if they did not exist.

Sometimes conflict is based on matters which can be changed. If negotiation is possible couples should consider it a major responsibility to work things out. Sometimes, however, conflict is based on basic character differences which are inseparable from the individual's personality. It may be impossible to change these, so if love is to survive or deepen more tolerance' will have to become part of the relationship. Each marriage will have its own kinds of conflicts; each resolution will have its own pattern.

One of the most overlooked aspects of Christian marriage is the role played by forgiveness within the process of marital interaction.[22] Forgiveness is not on the mind of couples when they first exchange marital vows. This may explain in part why it is not usually associated with the theology of

[21]*Ibid.,* p. 88.

[22]David M. Thomas, "Marital Forgiveness," *Marriage and Family Living* 62 (April, 1980), pp. 2-5.

marriage. Yet any analysis of the lived experience of couples will show that it exerts a significant influence. It is only after the days and years of marriage that *grounds* for forgiveness come into being.

If forgiveness is genuine it will come from the heart. If not, it will breed self-pity. Forgiveness also establishes a significant link between the processes of marriage enrichment and the religious values of the couple. True reconciliation is founded on an attitude of acceptance, an attitude more generous than required by simple justice. Forgiveness includes the willingness to accept whatever comes, even though it may be different from that which one prefers. Forgiveness of a person is an acceptance of qualities one may find naturally unattractive. To forgive in marriage requires that one move beyond the narrow categories of the acceptable to include everything which is genuinely a part of one's spouse, for better or worse. True forgiveness heals the hurts which are almost always a part of a living marital relationship.

When Jesus advocated forgiveness, many listened in disbelief. More in harmony with the human spirit seemed to be a sense of radical justice: an eye for an eye. Wasn't God only on the side of the good? When he first raised the issue of forgiveness the disciples had just been told that they were to be the gatekeepers of the Kingdom. Peter, in particular, was to have the keys. The practical question of the moment for Peter was who should be kept outside the gates. Jesus responded with the well-known formula of forgiveness seventy times seven. In other words, Peter shouldn't be concerned about who is to be kept out. Jesus taught him to be more concerned about who could be let in. Forgiveness was the key.

It takes a bigger person to forgive the sinner than to condemn one. And while this may appear to apply only to matters of salvation and judgment, I mention it here as a very practical way to be married as a Christian. Forgiveness is *the* Christian relational skill. When it is allowed to transform a particular human relationship it endows that relationship with God's life and power. Is that not part of why the New Testament speaks of marriage as reflecting God's covenantal attitude? The task is to take the rather abstract aspects of the Christian life and apply their meaning to the ordinary events of human life.

In the marriage vows, each promises to be accepting and caring of the other. The promise is *open*; it is an unconditional commitment to accept the other person without reserve. It is a huge risk because one can never predict what will happen in the years ahead. That is why Christian marriage cannot be limited to simple, contractual specifications. People simply don't make contracts with open clauses. In contracts matters have to be pinned-down in advance.

It would be deceitful, of course, to promise something one had no real intentions of fulfilling. That is why forgiveness is so central to an understanding of marriage as a sacrament. Many unanticipated events will happen; many features of one's marriage partner will surface which will cause surprise, worry, displeasure, even panic. When this happens, one may be tempted to turn the other way, to deny what is happening. But another option is to accept the unanticipated parts of the marriage as a special gift. This can be very hard; in fact, it can amount to the most difficult task imaginable. Remember in this context the image of the not-promised rose garden.

Does this mean that the goal of Christian marriage amounts to long-suffering acceptance of whatever comes to be? In the end, is passivity what is called for? No, that is not the point. A distinction between those matters which can be changed for the betterment of both wife and husband, and those matters which are an essential part of the person has to be made. Today our sense of the former category is growing. People can change, and the process can be helped by others who care and possess a good understanding of the human person.

Wife and husband are present to each other not only to comfort each other, but also to challenge one another to improve. Husbands and wives live in the tension of acceptance and challenge. Living out the tension is more of an art than a science. It is only done well where there coexists a great love for the person as well as a desire to facilitate all that the person might become.

To accomplish this requires a depth of mutual understanding which is, perhaps, not very common in contemporary marriages. To support change that is within the reach of a person, as distinct from a desired change which is unrealistic, requires a down-to-earth assessment of each other's potential. The judgment must be tailored to each concrete person. Imaginary scenarios drawn from the many "how to" books of the pop psychologists or sexologists often create frustration at best, or even total discouragement because the wife or husband fail to change according to the way the "experts" predicted.

It is often suggested that the major cause of marital difficulty is that too much is expected. This is partly true. Perfect marriages exist only in the pages of paperback novels. My own view is that expectations, in general, are not too high; they are rather misunderstood. We all can be better people. The question is whose definition of "better" are we to follow. God sees perfection in terms of love. And the kind of love that is best is one that is altruistic, generous, forgiving, and faithful. Perfect love is a possible goal in Christian marriage.

The source of that love is God and the more that married Christians are able to reach into that source for their life together, the more they will reach that potential God had in mind as each was created.

In the writings of Teilhard de Chardin, one finds two types of energy described. Both are forms of fire. The first type of energy is more common. It is the energy which comes from nature, usually from the burning of fuel. It is the power which moves our machines and transports us around the globe. The second type of fiery energy is more subtle in form, but more powerful in effect. In 1934, Teilhard wrote this:

> "The day will come when, after harnessing the ether (space), the winds, the tides, gravitation, we shall harness for God the energies of love. And, on that day, for the

second time in the history of the world, man will have discovered fire."[23]

The creation of this loving "fire" is central to the task of married Christians. It happens first in their love for each other as husband and wife. It extends beyond them as they assist God in bringing new life into being. God's love is a fertile love. And all love rooted in God's love, as conjugal love is, will also contain the quality of generativity. This topic is the focus of the next chapter.

[23]Teilhard de Chardin, *Toward the Future*, New York: Harcourt Brace Jovanovich, 1975, pp. 86-87.

CHAPTER VI:
BLESSED WITH CHILDREN

The biblical approach to children who are brought into this wide world is simply this: they are a gift from God, a blessing of immeasurable value. This is because they are persons endowed by the Creator with human *life*, a quality of being which flows directly from God, the source of all life.

Christian marriage is adequately described only when it is positioned as participating actively in the process of God loving humanity. A similar point must be made with reference to what Vatican II terms "the supreme gift of marriage," i.e., new life, which is created by Christian marital love,[1] Each person born into the world receives not only the gift of unmerited existence, but also receives a full measure of God's love. To facilitate the fullest possible experience of love, God masterfully designed marriage, including the interaction central to marriage, as expressive of love. The task of responding fully to God's high intent is far from easy, as has already been noted. Nevertheless, the creation of new life from love, a pattern essential to God's own creative activity, is one of the privileged ways we become, in small measure, imitators of God.

[1]Vatican II, *The Pastoral Constitution on the Church in the Modern World*, section 50.

Christian thought has traditionally spoken of this task as cooperating with God. Based on the fact that each person possesses the gift of immortality, the meaning of generation cannot be limited to human agency alone. Therefore, because God intentionally uses human activity as the means by which new life is brought into the world, true cooperation between God and the couple is correctly associated with procreation. With new biological procedures of creating life *in vitro* (outside the woman, or literally, "in a glass"), one wonders how far the process of creating new life can be extended without violating the essential link between love and life. While I will not discuss the matter here, it should be mentioned that any resolution of this issue requires an adequate description of marriage. An analysis of biological possibilities which consider only the physical aspect of the fetus is inadequate for it does not take into account that human life is created ultimately by a loving God.

In the last chapter we discussed life as it unfolded *in* the marital relationship. Here we will extend the discussion to include life as it comes *from* the relationship. The primary, although certainly not the only example of conjugal generativity, focuses upon the child, which begins its existence through the sexual embrace of the couple in marriage.

Recent Catholic thought, particularly as stated in Vatican II, maintains a firm connection between marital love and the procreation of new life. It also emphasizes (and here the tradition goes all the way back to Augustine's treatise on marriage) that procreation and education cannot be separated. In this chapter three significant instances of cooperating with God's creative love will be explored. First, the procreative dimensions of marriage will be presented along with some reflections of the sensitive topic of fertility control. Second, I will share some thoughts on the task of Christian parenting so as to clarify the role of parents as they not only assist God in creating new life, but also facilitate its return to its source in God. Finally, I will expand the notion of marital generativity to include other ways of cooperating with God's involvement in continuing creation, particularly as an ever fuller realization of the

Kingdom first initiated by Jesus. This will serve as a bridge to the next chapter which covers the spirituality and ministry proper to married Christians. The trajectory of this phase of the marital journey begins with that which is immediate, the couple itself, to that which is more external to those who take life from their union, their children. The journey is further extended, as it must be, to reach others who make up the membership of God's total family, all humanity.

Much has been made in recent years of the stages in human life as sketched in the writings of the well-known psychologist, Erik Erikson. After the challenges of human intimacy are resolved, hopefully in a healthy, positive manner, Erikson notes that the next task facing the person relates to generativity.[2] Understanding what it means to achieve a positive resolution of generativity is helped by knowing that failure is stagnation or self-absorption.

For most married Christians, generativity centers around conceiving, giving birth to, and nurturing their own children toward maturity. We also cannot forget those who adopt children into their family, or act as foster parents for the young. It is not automatic that parenting involves a positive resolution of generativity. Like all human acts, parenting is subject to potential sinfulness. To use the language of Erikson, instead of contributing positively to the next generation, one withholds personal giving through being overly concerned about oneself (self-absorption), or one does nothing much at all (stagnation). While in a position to offer something to posterity, one chooses instead to hoard one's resources. Both giver and receiver thereby lose a precious opportunity and the world is less for it.

We ought not to overlook the benefits which accrue to the generative person. Satisfaction secured through a job well done cannot be calculated in economic currency. Further, when the generativity is transpersonal, as is the case between

[2]See Erik H. Erikson, *Childhood and Society* (2nd edition), New York: W. W. Norton and Co., Inc., pp. 266-268. See also John J. Gleason, Jr., *Growing up to God,* Nashville: Abingdon Press, 1975, pp. 105-116.

parent and child, there is a process of reciprocity where the giving and the receiving are blended into a single pattern of enrichment for both. Parents often testify to the new sense of life gained by contributing to the growth of children. Wonder is experienced in the child as each new facet of the world is perceived. Such wonder has a way of spilling over to the parent. This can almost be called a revitalization process for the parent who is willing to spend the time and attention needed to enter into the world of the child or the teen.[3] While an earlier agrarian society may have considered the birth of a child as a blessing because this meant an added hand for the work on the farm, today's more industrialized or technologized society must look beyond economic benefits to appreciate the "blessing" associated with the child's entry into the family.

Today's benefits will be more personal and spiritual, which is not to deny that earlier eras failed to sense these same dimensions. Today blessings will flow particularly from the quality of the exchange between parent and child. Growth in parenting education is now seen as both valuable and needed. We are also recognizing those special contributions of the parent to the child's development, which are virtually irreplaceable by any other social agent. As society becomes more impersonal or functional, settings of genuine, caring personal contact become all the more precious. For the developing child, the unconditional acceptance, support and guidance of a loving parent provides not only the basis for healthy human growth, but also the foundation for religious maturation. For that reason Vatican II described the family as a "a kind of school of deeper humanity."[4]

A primary struggle for the next decade, at least, appears to be a conflict between the attitude of caring (the primary

---

[3]See David M. Thomas, "How Teens Raise Their Parents," *Marriage and Family Living*, 64 (January, 1982), pp. 10-13, 25.

[4]Vatican II, *Church in the Modern World*, section 52.

virtue of healthy generativity) and self-absorption.[5] Both dispositions can be present in the same person. We long for the illusive goal of self-fulfillment, while at the same time, we seek connectiveness or community. It is not necessary to judge these two stances as totally irreconcilable. A balanced concern for the self, and for one's neighbor is not an impossible achievement. It remains difficult, however, in a society saturated with a self-centered ethos, as ours is today. Important for each person, therefore, is an awareness of these basic attitudes so that in freedom, one can do what is best both for the self and for others, who have a need for one's attention and care.

The Value of Procreation

The primary value associated with procreation is *life*, new life brought into the world. While this may appear obvious, the motives for having children in today's world range from ones quite self-centered, to those of generous altruism.

Life is a gift from God, in fact, it is God's most singular gift. That is why we, who are privileged to assist God in creating human life, must also exert full personal responsibility in decisions which relate to procreation of new life. Its occurrence should not be left to chance, to blind fate. When the church describes the blessing inherent in parenthood, it does so consistently with the phrase "responsible parenthood." The decision to have a child should stem from a foundation of love: God's love for humanity coupled with the love of wife and husband. This love is rooted in freedom, in conscious decisions which make of us creative and caring Christians.

Discoveries in the life sciences have assisted us in making more responsible choices in these matters. It was not until the last century that we knew in detail the miraculous pro-

[5]See an excellent analysis of this in Daniel Yankelovich, *New Rules: Searching for Self-Fulfillment in a World Turned Upside Down*, New York: Random House, 1981.

cess by which the human ovum became fertilized by the human sperm to form human life in its initial stages. Awareness of the female fertility cycle, while known in its basics, is still being refined as new methods of inquiry are being developed. With each advance in our understanding of the procreative process, decisions with regard to creating life, or should conditions necessitate the opposite, preventing the conception of new life in a particular act of sexual intercourse, can become more responsible because they are more informed by fact.[6] Noteworthy is the church's support of continuing research in coming to a fuller understanding of the procreative process.

A responsible decision concerning the creation of new life demands serious personal reflection joined with honest and enlightened discussion between the wife and husband. It should be a shared decision. To decide responsibly involves consideration of the personal, social, economic and biological health of the existing family unit. It will take into account the needs of children already born in the family. It will be aware of the condition present in society outside the family.

Christian marital love includes as one of its essential characteristics the quality of fecundity. Stated clearly in his encyclical on responsible parenthood, Paul VI wrote, "...this love is *fecund* for it is not exhausted by the communion between husband wife, but is destined to continue raising up new lives."[7]

Belief in the *value* of new life is often rooted in a conviction that in its depth it is profoundly religious. The person of faith will look to affirm an acceptance of a fundamental goodness vested in creation *at all times*. The power of goodness is stronger than that of evil. Hope is more appropriate than pessimism or fatalism. In the words of John Paul II, "Against the pessimism and selfishness which casts a shadow over the world the church stands for life: in each

[6]See Paul VI, "On the Regulation of Birth", (Humanae Vitae), in *Love and Sexuality, Official Catholic Teachings,* section 10.

[7]*Ibid.,* section 9.

human life she sees the splendor of that 'yes,' that 'amen,' who is Christ himself."[8]

While the value of life itself is preeminent, other values deserve to be brought into the decision to have a child. A useful set of criteria for making this decision is provided by noted theologian Walter Kasper.[9] First, there must be respect for one's marriage partner and for the continual enrichment of the conjugal relationship. Second, consideration must be given for the children already a part of the family, their needs in the present and in the future. Third, attention to the needs of the wider society and the whole human race deserve consideration. And fourth, respect must be given to the inner meaning of human nature, a nature that ought not be exploited or manipulated for self-ish purposes. All these factors point to the fact that a decision is not to be made as if it were totally a private matter. While primary attention should derive from the love and the marriage of the couple, wider concerns also play a role. Further, since our humanity is given to us as a gift from God, a humanity designed to carry forward in history the life-giving love of God, we are not free to arbitrarily decide any actions. To quote the teaching of Vatican II:

> "Therefore when there is question of harmonizing conjugal love with the responsible transmission of life, the moral aspect of any procedure does not depend solely on sincere intentions or on an evaluation of motives. It must be determined by objective standards. These, based on the nature of the human person and his acts, preserve the full sense of mutual life-giving and human procreation in the context of true love."[10]

Based on this teaching, the matter of responsible parenthood involves both the option of having children, but also the selection of means toward achieving the desired goal.

[8]John Paul II, "On the Family," section 30.
[9]Walter Kasper, *The Theology of Christian Marriage*, p. 20
[10]Vatican II, *Church in the Modern World*, section 51.

The position of the Catholic Church is well known with regard to its prohibition of using artificial methods of limiting conception. The church's teaching is based on maintaining two meanings for sexual relations — the so-called unitive and procreative dimensions — in every expression of sexual intercourse in marriage. John Paul II recently submitted argumentation based on appreciation for the personalistic values at stake.

> "When couples, by means of recourse to contraception, separate these two meanings that God the creator has inscribed in the being of man and woman and in the dynamism of their sexual communion, they act as 'arbiters' of the divine plan and they 'manipulate' and degrade human sexuality and with it themselves and their married partner by altering its value of 'total' self-giving. Thus the innate language that expresses the total reciprocal self-giving of husband and wife is overlaid, through contraception, by an objectively contradictory language, namely, that of not giving oneself totally to the other. This leads not only to a positive refusal to be open to life, but also to a falsification of the inner truth of conjugal love, which is called upon to give itself in personal totality."[11]

I have provided the full quote of John Paul II to emphasize that the foundation for the church's stance is intended as a support for the value of the person, or more to the point, for the dynamics of the *interpersonal* sexual encounter in Christian marriage. The language of natural law, more common in earlier formulations prohibiting artificial contraception, has been augmented by personalistic framework, which is more in line with contemporary thought.

Most important to note is the manner in which the issue related to healthy conjugal love. The principle of responsible birth control, based on the shared decision of the couple, has been a part of the accepted teaching of the Catholic

[11]John Paul II, "On the Family," section 32.

Church since Pius XII.[12] A couple is not asked to bring as many children into the world as are biologically possible. What's needed, however, is an understanding as to how the value of both conjugal love and procreation are interrelated, and how the use of artificial contraception violates their unity. John Paul II argues that the two meanings are related to the *totality* essential to an understanding of conjugal sex.

Interpersonal manipulation, the mere use of another as an object, is the disvalue being denounced. It is argued that the use of natural family planning, which respects the periods of fertility and infertility inherent in the reproductive cycle, protects personal integrity. The use of NFP, as it is usually referred to, respects such values as the cooperation between wife and husband, a certain discipline in controlling human response, and a quest for expressing sexual love in other ways besides sexual intercourse. Effective use of NFP calls forth a practical spirituality which encompasses the whole marriage, not just its sexual dimension. It is not simply a birth control procedure, and perhaps the lack of widespread acceptance of NFP is related somewhat to the hedonistic society of today, a society which places instant gratification ahead of other values needed for the type of ascetism required by NFP.

This issue of morality cannot be simply limited to the choice of approved methods. A deeper issue concerns the responsible transmission of life within the framework of the vitality of the marital relationship. One might employ a perfectly acceptable procedure from the standpoint of the authoritative church teaching, but do so selfishly or without due regard for one's spouse.[13] This would be immoral. The decision associated with generously and genuinely responding to the values inherent in the procreative dimension of Christian marriage involves a cluster of values. That conscientious couples often agonize over this matter is certainly true. Yet, once informed of the church's total teaching, and

[12]Pius XII, Discourse of Oct. 29, 1951, *A.A.S.* 43 (1951), pp. 835-854.

[13]See Bernard Haring, *Free and Faithful in Christ*, Vol. II, New York: The Seabury Press, 1979, pp. 523 — 530.

aware of the values supported by that teaching, each couple before God is entrusted with making an appropriate response.

That many Catholics fail to follow in practice the current teaching of the church with regard to the use of artificial contraception is of serious pastoral concern. At the Synod of Bishops meeting in Rome in 1980, Archbishop John R. Quinn addressed the assembly on behalf of the National Conference of Catholic Bishops in the United States.[14] While not calling into question the fundamental correctness of the church's teaching, he asked for further research and discussion to create a better formulation and argumentation for the church's position. He referred to a recent, well-respected national study which pointed out that the majority of Catholic women use birth control methods condemned by Paul VI's Encyclical. The Archbishop called for an international dialogue among theologians to deepen the church's understanding of the issue and to develop the teaching in the context of a positive theology of human sexuality and marital intimacy.

Also important to recall is the pastoral sensitivity present in the church with regard to this teaching. The difficulty associated with an explicit following of the teaching is clearly acknowledged. Mention of the availability of God's generous forgiveness is usually referred to when the topic is presented. In summary, the values at stake are: the value of life itself, the importance of maintaining conjugal love, the need for mutual respect of persons, reverence for the human person and those aspects of human response which have been invested in our nature by God's wonderous handiwork. The church's teaching flows from fundamental Gospel values, those of love, peace, freedom, and joy. Any teaching on contraception cannot be at odds with this spirit. Rather it must exemplify it.

The procreative aspect of Christian marriage is intrinsically related to the love between wife and husband. Their

---

[14]John R. Quinn, "Contraception: A Proposal for the Synod," *Origins* 10 (Oct. 16, 1980).

love is creative both of each other, and of persons who may issue from their love. New life requires attention and care, particularly in its early stages of development. Therefore, the procreative value demands the complementary value of what is usually termed in formal church teachings, "education." The word unfortunately can be misleading because of its association with formal schooling. If one remembers, however, the original Latin root of the word, its meaning involves "leading one out into the world." With that understanding we can begin to grasp more adequately the proper meaning of the concept, as well as the wide range of its implications.

Christian Reflections on Parenting

While we cannot have recourse to an eyewitness account of God's original creation of the universe, most traditional Christians who thought about this event, took literally the words of Genesis, i.e., that the whole effort took no longer than six days to accomplish. Then, like any worker after six days of work, God took a day off and rested. And as far as it was imagined, if it was thought about at all, God was still resting.

Recent theological speculation, however, moves in a different direction by affirming that not only is God not at rest, but that the work of creation is still taking place. The concept of "continuing creation" is widely accepted as our appreciation grows of the various processes at work in forming the world. The general outline of Teilhard de Chardin, while debated in many particulars, is helpful. Teilhard pointed out that the processes of creation are largely focused today on mental and social development with the corresponding transformation of those structures of creation most related to growing understanding and love. Contrary processes are also certainly in evidence, a fact often admitted by Teilhard himself. But the power of God, he optimistically believed, contained superior energy for insuring ultimate victory, a victory first celebrated in the Resurrection of the Christ.

I initiate the discussion of parenting with a reflection on creation theology to point out how the process of parenting corresponds to the process involved in God's continuing creation. In fact, parenting is an important part of the on-going creation of the world.

Reflect on the words of John Paul II to parents: "The task of giving education is rooted in the primary vocation of married couples to participate in God's creative activity: By begetting in love and for love a new person who has within himself or herself the vocation for growth and development, parents by that very fact take the task of helping that person effectively to live a fully human life."[15]

Each person is created out of love. Each one is created to love. As has been mentioned often throughout this book, love demands concrete expression if it is to be genuinely human. And unless it is human, it cannot be thought of as Christian. The love affair between parent and child, while lifelong in duration, will be expressed in different ways depending on the needs of the child — and also of the parent. Sensitive judgment is necessary to interpret the best way to love: to blend the right proportion of assistance, guidance, and "letting-go" so that the journey toward maturity is given a good start.[16]

Two cultural emphases positively assist a deeper realization of Christian parenting today. First, there is a greater valuing of interpersonal life, and second, we find increased attention directed toward the developmental stages of life. The parent-child relationship is clearly both interpersonal and developmental. Its laws of growth and success are nuanced by an appreciation of the intricacies embodied in the relation of a very particular parent with a very unique child. General laws of parenting can only be generally applied. Room must always be made by wise parents for what

---

[15]John Paul II, "On the Family," section 36.

[16]What follows is based on my own "Toward and Theology of Christian Parenting," in *Christian Parenting*, New York: Paulist Press, 1980, pp. 11-14.

is special in their relationship with each child. Parent and children are persons, not things, or what would be even worse, interchangeable parts of a machine. Further, the sense of the different needs of children *and parents* at different moments of their lives also contributes its own set of insights into this most demanding and rewarding relationship. Properly understood, the act of parenting will be taken lightly by none. It will call forth for the parent what's best in their humanity and what's central to their lives as Christians.

While many voices have been, and continue to be heard as to the human side of parenting, it is doubtful that many Christians are aware of developments in theological circles which can aid them in their personal understanding of parenting. Excellent ideas have circulated of late and what follows is a survey of these ideas with the intent that they will also be related to the actual experiences of Christian parents.

Expressions in the church which establish both the dignity and task of the Christian parent refer to the Christian family as "the Domestic Church" or "the Church of the Home." This approach to the Christian significance of the family is much more than a pious or spiritual way of speaking. It touches every facet of the Christian family as it participates in God's salvation of humanity. *For most, the life of the Christian family is their first, most direct, most influential, and most on-going experience of God's salvific love.* It will be a setting for their personal encounter with God's faithful and forgiving love. The Christian community of the family has privileged status in the ordinary/extraordinary affairs between God and humanity.

The Christian family concretizes in its daily life the power of the Lord to save and sanctify. This is done particularly through the ennobled interaction of parent with child, described by Vatican II as "the first to communicate the faith to their children."[17] The faith dimension of life is communicated by both word and deed. But most of all it is through

[17]Vatican II, *Decree on the Apostolate of the Laity,* section 11.

parental love which makes present for the child the care and continuous concern of God. The child is able to perceive, however dimly at first, that life's meaning is love and that a loving concern stands at the beginning of all life. Therefore, parental love can be appreciated as *foundational* for receiving both the gift and experience of Christian faith. Christian parental love makes sense in light of its support from the God who loves without conditions, as it is strengthened to "go that extra mile" because it is rooted in the generosity of God.

This quality of life within the Christian family merits the Church's highest regard and its fullest support. Vatican II has described this setting as "the domestic sanctuary of the Church."[18] It should not be imagined that the council had in mind some perfectly organized and smoothly functioning family unit. The danger of using vocabulary like "sanctuary" or "church" is that these words generate images of order, tranquility, quiet and rest, which are hardly everyday qualities of normal family life. In using church images the intent is definitely to expand their range so that they will include many of the very mundane and messy features of real life. The "church" described, when it is given a family reference, is the "church" of runny noses, dirty diapers, cluttered kitchens, finger-printed walls, confused schedules and ruffled nerves. It is out of that raw material that the "Church of the Home" is created. Granted this is probably perceived as a rather broad extension of the principle of sacramentality — the theological principle which describes the presence and life of God in creation — but it is an extension very necessary to point to the fact that God is present in reality! One might recall in this context that many eye-witnesses of Jesus found difficulty in accepting him because he appeared so ordinary. They also had difficulty in relating to some of his very "ordinary" friends.

In the specific context of parenting this also means that one's Christian parenting will include much more than what might narrowly be construed as religiously significant.

[18] *Ibid.*

While normal religious education is a side of parenting most will consider as the basic task of Christian parents (and it is quite important), other dimensions of parenting are equally serious. Recall that the context for Christian parenting is the full life of the person. This approach is comprehensive. And as it is better understood and appreciated, it will reach out to include everything of significance as it relates to the generation of full Christian personhood.

Being rooted in all of life, Christian parenting will experience the shortcomings and weaknesses of all that we have come to describe as the human condition. It will know moments of failure and utter frustration. It will experience times of doubt and despair. It will even tell of times when the challenge of love seemed too much. And like other areas of human life, there will be times when sins of commission or omission will be confessed. So the Christian parent will need forgiveness. And God is always ready to forgive.

As has already been noted the most common word used in describing the role of Christian parents is that of education. But it must be noted that they are educators in a very special sense of that word. Their educational responsibility extends into their responsibility for both the personal and social growth of their children, a role so central that Vatican II states that "scarcely anything can compensate for their failure in it."[19] Again, this points to the broad meaning of parenting when it is grasped in a Christian framework. This education touches particularly on the social or relational development of the child. Rosemary Haughton is moved to describe the goal of the Christian family in clear relational terms. She writes: "The purpose of the family is for the formation of people who are able to love."[20] That ability, of course, is not self-generated. It is based on the experience of being loved and accepted by those one considers important. And in most cases, this will involve the experience of parental love.

[19]Vatican II, *Declaration on Christian Education,* section 3.

[20]Rosemary Haughton, *Problems of Christian Marriage,* New York: Paulist Press, 1968, p. 21.

In this rich human milieu, where the reality of love is known and experienced, where persons are accepted not only for what they accomplish, but more deeply, for who they are, the effective telling of the story of God's love can occur — and it can be understood! For this reason the council described the Christian family as the Domestic Church where parents are "the first preachers of the faith to their children."[21]

In imparting an awareness of the Good News of Jesus to their children, parents also move to a deeper participation themselves in the mystery of God's faithful love. Their role is one of dignity and grace. Their parenthood encompasses true acts of co-operation with God in the procreation of new life and also in enhancing the life of grace in their children. What rises to the surface is a tremendous sense of life in all its miraculous forms. The family becomes the cell of life for both the Church and society. And while it can be argued that parents are simply part of the web of life within the family, it can also be asserted that they stand as initiators of that life as they respond to the wellspring of all life in God.

It follows that Christian marital and parental love is, above all, a creative love. It is altruistic and enriching of others. By its very nature it includes both the presence of love and the valuing of life. In fact, the love itself is generative of new life. As Vatican II put it: "Marriage and conjugal love are by their nature ordained toward the begetting and education of children."[22]

By stating that it is conjugal love itself, rather than simply the biological union of the couple, which is creative of new life, the council boldly broke new ground. In essence it is declaring that it is the personal union of the couple which God uses as the vehicle for creating new human life. The parents' love for each other has more than simple human or psychological value; it is of immense spiritual value.

This understanding of the spiritual is quite incarnational.

---

[21]Vatican II, *Dogmatic Constitution on the Church*, section 11.

[22]Vatican II, *Church in the Modern World*, section 50.

It speaks of God's creative power present in the human loving acts of wife and husband. In their mutual expressions of love, which are not restricted to expressions through sexual intercourse, the couple is touched by God. And through their love, the love of God gains new earthly expression, especially for the little ones as they come to be and as they become themselves responsible persons.

Just as it takes both parents to create new life, we seem to appreciate more clearly today the role of both parents in child development. As both parents communicate to the child a sense of significance, they draw from the child some of its own unique and personal gifts. The child's growing sense of his or her sexual identity is also the result of parental contact. There is even some evidence that the role of the father in the religious development of his children merits greater attention than previously supposed when the mother was seen as the primary agent of religious growth. What all this says is that it is difficult to over-estimate the impact of the parents on the total development of the person of the child. This is not to conclude that parental influence is totally deterministic of the outcome of the child's fate. We remain, after all, free persons throughout life. And we are becoming more sensitive to rather significant stages of human growth into and throughout adult life. But the influence of the parents is fundamental, or better, foundational in that it influences later development by fostering certain possibilities and curtailing others.

A parent's role is foundational for both human and Christian development. While God's grace is an influence of great power, capable of overcoming any created obstacle save the hardened and closed heart of the sinner, God's influence will nevertheless be felt through the human situation. The eventual shape of one's Christian life will feel the influence of early life experiences, which are largely parent-child events. The phrase, therefore, that parents are the primary religious educators of their children is almost a truism particularly if you take primary to mean foundational. The parent's influence is felt whether there is specific advertance or not. Education takes place even in silence. Of course, if a parent desires to be a responsible parent in this regard, he or she will be concerned about the content of both their words and deeds, all of which become "lessons" in the school of faith which is the Christian family.

What results from these ideas about Christian parenting is a deep appreciation of the parent-child connection as a forge in which the very being of the human person is first fired. Parenting becomes an expression of both human and Christian creativity as it eminates from the creative love of God for each person. While it is all too common that we dwell on the failures and foibles of contemporary parents, it is also useful to point to the good things which are happening in families as parents look more responsibly to their task of nurturing the personhood of their children. With the growth of parenting programs and practical literature in the art and science of parenting, parents need not feel as unsupported by good advice as they might have been in the past. There is also a growing awareness of the pluralistic context of parenting with special needs acknowledged for the single parent, the parent of handicapped children, or for the parent of meager resources either economic or otherwise.

Family life, if genuinely Christian, will typically manifest particular contours. It will resemble that kind of life which was exemplified most perfectly by Jesus. The child will learn from the parent what it means to be loving of another. Embedded in the child will be a sense of self-worth which is spawned by the acceptance given by the parent. That acceptance is ultimately based on the parent's sense that the child is a gift from God who loves that same child without reservation. The parent seeks to replicate that divine disposition to the child in ways that meet the child's need for acceptance at each stage of development. This is not to be interpreted as a simple attitude of permissiveness; the acceptance is focused on the person, and not on the many forms of behavior which may or may not develop from what is best in that person. In other words, the parent can and must be critical of the child from time to time. There is a confrontational and challenging side to Christian parental love — just as there is in God's love.

Much of this discussion has been, of necessity, general. This is because of the uniqueness of each relationship between parent and child. It is up to the insights and evaluations of the parent — and sometimes of the child as well —to translate these theological principles into everyday living. In their encounters then, there will be realized a bit more of that Kingdom promised by God and described by Jesus as already present in the love within the Christian family.

Other Expressions of Life-Giving

The generative expression of Christian marriage, while ordinarily focused on the many actions associated with parenting, has other very important dimensions. There are many couples who are infertile because of biological inability to have children. Estimates put their number at close to 10% of existing marriages. Many couples adopt children. Others, however, choose to express their life-giving, life-enriching capacities in ways other than parenting.

Generosity toward projects which improve the life of humanity, toward research requiring great expenditures of time and effort, or toward the care of family members (for instance, aged or invalid parents), are examples of creative accomplishment on behalf of others.

Whatever the expression of generativity, its source should be the generosity of caring for others rather than self-absorption, to borrow again from the language of Erikson. I have already suggested that parenting is capable of association with all the wrong motives and patterns of behavior. Children can be "used" to accomplish self-centered parental goals.

The same tension exists in non-parental examples of generativity. Projects can be done simply to acquire personal wealth, power, or reputation. Contributing to subsequent generations may have little, or absolutely nothing, to do with one's activities. The desire for power need not, however, be judged as destructive. In fact, power may be viewed as a necessary prerequisite for acccomplishing significant good. It is only the misuse of power that deserves condemnation. Power is an essential part of generativity.

God is sometimes described as all powerful. The Spirit of God "comes" to share God's power with humanity for the renewal of the earth, for the building of the Kingdom of God in its terrestrial form. A major theme in the writings of St. Paul concerns the way God's power is transferred into the Christian community as a force for good. Works of healing, of converting people's lives to God are interpreted as manifestations of power. Generativity, as we have been discussing it throughout this chapter, is the power to create and nurture life. The enrichment of existing life, or the destruction of those forces which impede a fuller realization of life, as it is discussed, for instance, in Liberation Theology, express the generativity of God as it takes form through human agency. God's desire to see humanity reach its rightful status as fully alive requires that each person, each married couple, each family become more life-creative and life-nurturing.

This orientation toward life ought not be kept within the marital or even the family community. Unless these social units perceive a mission broader than simply their own survival, they will halt the spread of God's love, a task entrusted to each Christian community, however small its membership may be. In our society, which has tendencies toward quite limited or narcissistic interests, a conscious effort must be made to reach out to the extended family, to neighbors and to others, particularly if they are in need.[23] The Gospel mandate to work for peace and justice, both within the family and with all the communities which the family touches (which is virtually all communities in our era of global interdependence), is a task incumbent upon all Christian families.[24]

[23]See Christopher Lasch, *The Culture of Narcissism,* New York: W. W. Norton and Co., 1978.

[24]See Kathleen and James McGinnis, *Parenting for Peace and Justice*, Maryknoll: Orbis Books, 1981.

What Christian marriage and family life need today is an outgoing spirituality and expression of ministry consonant with their particular status in society and in the church. It should be a spirituality and ministry thoroughly Christian, yet responsive to their uniqueness. One that is simply borrowed from other types of religious life is of little value. Today, married Christians are beginning to have more of a voice in both the formal and informal structures of the church. While their contribution may be only in its early stages, their words exhibit a certain self-confidence born of a sense that the Spirit of the Lord is working through Christian marriage and family life at a level quite unlike previous times. This accomplishment is timely because the general trends in society are not particularly pro-marriage or pro-family.[25]

---

[25]See the report on the White House Conference on Families, *Listening to America's Families*, Washington: U. S. Government Printing Office, 1980.

CHAPTER VII:
DEEPENED BY
SPIRITUALITY

For some married Christians much of the church's traditional legalistic approach to marriage is disdainful. Endless discussions of the legal requirements for entering marriage, joined with abstract descriptions of a seemingly complex process for annulments, leave the impression that the theology of marriage has little to say about the ordinary vicissitudes of married life. Unfortunately, most married Christians have not been given the opportunity to reflect upon the riches of Christian insight relating to the spiritual life. It is in that area of religious thought where one's daily life is brought into the light of God's immense love. It translates the lofty-sounding words of formal theology into the language of ordinary life. Interest in spirituality is sadly thought by some to be reserved for ordained priests or vowed religious. A ruinous dicotomy is then allowed to develop between those who are interested in the spiritual life, and those who were only concerned with the things of the world.

By drawing attention to marital spirituality and ministry, I am adding necessary elements to compensate for the narrowness caused by legalistic descriptions. Whereas a legal approach is primarily concerned with what *minimum* factors are required to delineate Christian marriage, marital spirituality and ministry provides a sense of Christian marriage relating to the *maximum*, an orientation much more in harmony with the spirit of the Gospel.

The human potential movement regularly points out that most people fail to realize their full potential as persons. In furnishing suggestions and exercises designed to surface and activate dormant areas of the self, the movement aims at fostering a richer bounty of experience. Somewhat the same can be said here in relation to the untapped potential for spiritual growth for married Christians. But helpful in this pursuit is a good map to identify the location of the wealth. A comparison with a geology map is useful because it helps to reveal resources which lie hidden to the human eye, riches lying beneath the surface that are as real as anything on the surface. To perceive within a person all the God-given beauty, significance and value requires an awareness nourished by a vision of faith. An appreciation of the ordinary and mundane activities of daily married and family life as *important* for the building of the Kingdom of God requires a sense of God's hidden ways. Good theological maps help people see the veiled real presence of God in every good event of every day, whether the sun is shining or not.[1]

All things considered, the most important part of Christian marriage is its spiritual dimension which, while often overlooked, has a long-standing tradition in Christian thought. In the theology of Thomas Aquinas, for instance, the most excellent quality of marriage lies in its role in the supernatural or spiritual life.[2] This same theme is echoed in the first major papal treatise on Christian marriage in the twentieth century in which Pius XI wrote the following: "This mutual inward molding of husband and wife, this determined effort to perfect each other, can in a real sense,

[1]See the excellent contribution to this conversation by Dolores Leckey, *The Ordinary Way: A Family Spirituality*, New York: Crossroads Books, 1982.

[2]Thomas Aquinas. *Commentary on the Sentences*, 31. See also Bernard Lonergan, "Finality, Love and Marriage," pp. 18 - 22.

as the Roman Catechism teaches, be said to be the chief reason and purpose of matrimony..."[3] Genuine sanctity is just as possible for the married as for anyone else, although the official role of saints within the Catholic Church records not a single example of a person being canonized *because* of the quality of his or her married life. There are canonized married saints, but the record shows that they were officially inscribed as saints for accomplishments other than witnessing to the fullness of the Christian life in marriage. This is further evidence of a lack of sensitivity to the unique contribution married Christians make to the building of the Kingdom of God.

In recent years, however, there has been a growing awareness of a spirituality proper to married Christians. A significant advance is indicated in Vatican II's Dogmatic Constitution on the Church: "Married couples and Christian parents should follow their own proper path to holiness by faithful love, sustaining one another in grace throughout the entire length of their lives."[4] Much the same idea is repeated by Paul VI in a profound address given to the members of an international group dedicated to the development of a conjugal spirituality. In concise and clear language he affirmed, "Like all who are baptized, you are, in fact, called to holiness... But you should pursue that objective in your own manner, in and through your life as couples."[5]

But what is the "proper path" of spirituality for married Christians? What is the proper "manner" through which their spirituality unfolds? What does it mean to pursue the spiritual life "as couples?" While a review of the formal literature of theology and spirituality offers little guidance in this area, it should not be concluded that marital spirituality does not exist. It simply has not developed to any extent in published materials.

[3]Pius XI, "On Christian Marriage," 50.

[4]Vatican II, "Dogmatic Constitution on the Church," 41.

[5]Paul VI, "Address to the Teams of Our Lady," (May 4, 1970), 1.

What I offer here, therefore, should be read in the spirit of encouraging reflection, discussion, and clarification, particularly for married Christians. As a memory aid, I present suggestions according to the first few letters of the alphabet. While not attempting to provide a totally comprehensive picture, I believe that these qualities of spirituality deserve inclusion on a basic map of married spirituality: a foundation of *acceptance*, the inclusion of *basics*, the presence of the *cross*, a *diatic* or *dialogic* structure, the style of *earthiness* and the spirit of *fidelity*.[6] Because of the wide-ranging nature of marriage and family life, given the time and space, I could extend this list all the way to the importance of zeal, zest, or zip in conjugal spirituality. But here I conclude with the virtue of fidelity which in some sense can be creatively viewed as a primary orientation which underlies all the rest.

A Foundation of Acceptance

Marital spirituality, like all expressions of Christian spirituality, begins with witnessing to God's accepting and forgiving love. In marriage, this is first asserted *within* the marital relationship. Then, it is extended toward one's children, and moves outward in ever widening circles to include all humanity. Accepting love stands at the center of Christian spirituality as its authenticity is tested by love of neighbor. Absense of love of one's neighbor is a sure indication that one's spirituality is superficial, ethereal, and only theoretical. Jesus constantly noted that the presence of the Kingdom was revealed through the acts of kindness, service, and forgiveness. Jesus, himself, epitomized these acts, giving tangible evidence of God's love. Those who see themselves as followers of this man, are invited, or better, required, to do the same.

Acceptance is a fundamental quality in Christian love of neighbor. It takes its spirit from God's free and absolutely generous acceptance of each person. Marital and family

[6]See also my article, "Downhome Spirituality for Ordinary Families," *Studies in Formative Spirituality*, II:3 (Nov. 1981), pp. 447 - 459.

spirituality begins with accepting one's wife or husband, and the children with whom they are blessed, with full awareness of the uniqueness and particularity of each. Genuine Christian acceptance is not fickle or arbitrary. It does not change with varying moods. It does not run hot and cold. Being clearly human, it will be tested by shifting emotions, but its roots will be effectively set in imitation of God's pervasive acceptance. This kind of acceptance is as difficult a task as is humanly conceivable. What renders it all the more demanding is that one's acceptance is filled with a knowledge of real people with all their obvious faults and limitations.

Also part of God's acceptance is the added dimension of forgiveness. God is open to re-establish bonds of familial relationship even after family members have squandered their gifts and wasted the family inheritance. With open arms, so to speak, God patiently awaits a return, even hounding the profligate to come back home. To some, the logic of God's attitude and behaviour may seem ridiculous, even foolhardy.

God's acceptance takes each person as she or he is. It is rooted in a magnificent freedom, capable of transcending or going beyond all limitations. It is a quality which God shares with all who strive to live and to relate to others in a similar way. And while all this may seem to some rather abstract, it can be translated into a dynamic and revolutionary attitude which becomes the bedrock for marital spirituality.

In an earlier chapter I suggested how forgiveness provides a practical strategy for marriage enrichment. Forgiveness is another word for acceptance, with the added note that the accepting person is invited to become more large-hearted in affirming aspects of the marriage partner, perhaps unknown, perhaps not even present, at an earlier period in the marriage.

We touch here one of the most sensitive areas of marital life. Some marriages fail, with the causes of failure being many. Whether a more generous attitude of acceptance might save a marriage which eventually ends in separation or divorce is a matter answerable only by the individuals directly involved and by God who sees into the deepest thoughts. Acceptance, on the other hand, may serve to prevent a breakdown, and thereby become a key dynamic of marital enhancement.

It is the nature of vital interpersonal life to decline unless it is regularly nourished or enriched. Each marriage is filled with creative possibilities. Whether any creative potential is realized depends on how the uniqueness of each person is called forth into life. The most effective invitation is based on presumed acceptance of someone who knows and loves us.

Today's social environment is very restrictive of what it values. Take, for instance, the matter of personal appearance. The shape of one's body, the style of one's hair, the clothes one chooses are all subject to an evaluation process controlled by outsiders: the media, the advertisers, the trendy people. If an individual either cannot or will not conform to the prevailing shapes and styles ordained by the secular culture, that person may feel somewhat "unacceptable." Self-esteem can be undermined with the result that one may begin a program of activities whose sole purpose is to bring one into conformity with the prevailing images of acceptability. While this frenetic desire for acceptance according to group standards is usually associated with adolescents, it is also experienced within the adult world.

What is particularly tragic about the compulsive search for acceptance by a faceless society is that it may just be compensation for an absence of acceptance on the part of people who should know and care most: one's own family or one's marriage partner.

In marriage, acceptance is a day-by-day affair. It can usually be presumed that genuine love exists between the wife and husband at the time of the wedding. Acceptance will be particularly valuable as the unique personality and interests of each partner surfaces in their shared journey through life. Acceptance is as much an attitude as it is a specific act. Ideally, each is *open* to receive with open arms and a generous spirit the unrevealed qualities of the other. Part of the normal pattern will be judgment of specific shortcomings and displeasure over certain unanticipated and undesirable features of one's spouse. There can and should be mutual correction flowing from a loving concern. Almost no other area of marital exchange demands such delicacy and sensitivity. Awareness of one's own motives are necessary so that judgments and suggestions are supportive of healthy growth, and are not simply manipulative, based on self-centered interests. A similar sensitivity is needed by parents in judging their own children as well.

Reserved to God alone is the ability to judge the moral character of a person. Jesus was very clear that the judgment of sinfulness is proper to God alone. No human is empowered to render an assessment of the moral rightness or wrongness of anyone. Because of the intimacy characteristic of marriage, and because those who love deeply desire what's best for the beloved, it is all too common that spouses become acutely judgmental of each other, even extending assessment into the area of the spiritual. And the more serious one becomes about spirituality, the greater the tendency to judge the other in religious matters. These judgments are inappropriate; they overstep one's capacities and they serve neither God nor the persons involved. No human can gain the proper vantage point from which to make a judgment that can only be made by God. Self-righteousness often results from being judgmental and this can seriously erode a marriage. There is little defense against its destructive influence.

Marital love is often experienced as beyond reason or explanation. It is sometimes said by outsiders that what a particular wife or husband see in each other defies understanding. Maybe this is an indication of the almost limitless possibilities of the human spirit. Maybe it is the result of God's assisting grace. Most probably, it is the result of both.

The Inclusion Of Basics

Marital spirituality takes as its raw material the basic events of married life, seeing and living them as the essential ingredients of holiness. While some place spirituality in the realm of the esoteric or the unusual, mainline Christianity combines a belief in the goodness of creation with the power brought by Jesus in his incarnation to affirm the basic redemptive potential of *all* life. The range of God's interest is both extensive (all persons and things and their connections) and intensive (every aspect of all persons and things and their connections).

God created the universe with a word and a dream. God, aware of the risk, invited the cooperation of free persons in actualizing the dream. The door was left open for sharing or disdaining the dream.

In marriage the dream for creation is realized as wife and husband work and play to create a community of mutual love, a love powerful enough to be creative of new life. Yet that goal, that miraculous creation of wife, husband, and God, cannot be achieved in a moment, or in a single act. It results from countless acts that, when joined together, constitute a Christian marriage. The goal is the composite result of desire, intention, action, and response, repeated over and over again, with each time being somewhat different because of the way each person changes in time.

Spirituality in marriage is deeply interpersonal. It involves a response to God and to one's spouse with the unified response being a single act. One not only loves God *and* one's mate; one also loves God *in* one's mate. And there is no time of the day or night when the joining of those two fundamental loves is inappropriate.

Is it possible to love one's spouse too much? Not really, but it is conceivable to love in a distorted manner. Love, like any other human sentiment, can be unhealthy. This was noted in chapter 2. A distorted love can enslave both the lover and the beloved. A love that is not fully founded on freedom, or does not allow the other to live freely, is not the kind of love advocated by God. Marital love, as a created extension of God's love, will fall short of its sublime potential if it is not love freeing both the lover and the beloved.

Love is also impoverished if it is not translated into deed. In marriage the deeds of love are elemental. They are those actions which, to paraphrase a contemporary song lyric, help one make it through the day and night. Therefore, marital spirituality includes everything from the making of a good cup of coffee to the most demanding efforts of maintaining fidelity and daily concern for one's partner.

Sensitive marital spirituality will not be circumscribed by narrow "rules" of individual roles, but will always keep the needs of the person to whom one is married in the foreground. It will be a spirituality of humility which regards no task in marriage as beneath oneself, because the grandeur of the act comes not so much from what is done, as from the spirit in which it is done.

The concern of many Gospel passages, which tell us about feeding the hungry, giving drink to the thirsty, and clothing the naked, take on new meaning when applied to everyday marital life. The so-called functional needs met by marriage may not be the same for a couple who work long hours keeping the family farm going, as they would be for the two pay-check family who live in a high-rise condominium. But the need for personal acceptance, recognition, support and loving concern are much the same for all. And it is toward the meeting of these basic needs that a responsive marital spirituality moves.

Ministry in marriage, defined as the manner in which one's spirituality is outwardly expressed, will certainly be concerned with basics as well. For too long ministry has been thought of as pertaining only to religious or church-related activities. It has not been sufficiently appreciated as pertaining to the realm of the intimate and the everyday. The ministry of creating community is as central to Christianity as is any other expression of the Christian life. In marriage the many human expressions of endearment, service, and sacrifice are ministry in the full sense of that word. They embody the caring of God for each person, whether the person is fully conscious of that fact or not. This is one of the most important features of Christian marriage as a sacrament, a point that will be more fully developed in the next chapter. Matrimony is a sacrament of creation which means that it arises from the human dynamics of interpersonal life itself. This is the way God's activity enters the marriage. God's love and power become real through the love and courage and commitment of the couple.

Occasionally, marital spirituality takes on heroic expression when particular married people are required to deal with rather difficult situations, e.g., an alcoholic spouse, handicapped children, the whole spectrum of diseases both physical and mental which may effect marital life. Individuals who survive, even flourish in face of these difficulties, are holy in all senses of that term. Also worth noting is the spiritual value of the routine activities of marriage. A while back many Christians were alerted to a new meaning of holiness through reading the autobiography of a simple Carmelite nun, Therese of Lisieux, who found the opportunity for an intensive spiritual life within the confines of the ordinary routine of a cloistered convent. Similar accounts of ordinary holiness as it is lived out everyday in walk-up apartments, in split-level suburban dwellings, or in rural farm houses would be helpful for married Christians. Sanctity is created whenever the married, by the quality of their interpersonal life, transform matter into spirit, or bring that which was separate into relationship.

The Presence of the Cross

In a society bent on self-fulfillment, the idea of personal sacrifice on behalf of others is hardly a popular concept. In the widely read treatise on contemporary conjugal life, *Open Marriage*, neither the word nor the idea of sacrifice is to be found in its pages. The rigors of maintaining a marital relationship are side-stepped by strategies which encourage compensatory extramarital activity. If one's marriage partner is unable to meet one's needs, someone else is invited into one's life. Thus the marriage is "opened" to outsiders. What this does to basic values like commitment or fidelity is not discussed.

The Christian story of the death of Jesus is recorded against the background of his passion. The joining of passion and suffering with death provides an insight into the meaning of his whole life and the love which stands behind it. Passion is usually associated only with physical pain or endurance. It may be more helpful, however, to think of passion as a receptive orientation of the person toward others, which allows others to influence the direction of one's journey. An often-used phrase to summarize Jesus' life is that he is "a man for others." In that description we perceive in him an openness to others, to hearing their words and seeing their pain and joy. He is a listener, an observer. But his perceptions are not without personal involvement because he cares intensely about the people he encounters, desiring to meet their deepest needs whenever possible. The Latin root of passion, *passio*, means to allow oneself to be affected, to become passive in life to others. Through passion, one becomes vulnerable, accessible, and open to life.

It should be noted that this attitude exposes one to possible hurt and harm. Healthy mutual love is the only way which makes this kind of vulnerability valuable. Clearly a paradox exists here, the same paradox which is often pointed to in the New Testament: a mystery which turns giving into receiving, dying into life. Like all true paradoxes, it is not resolved by logical argumentation. It only makes sense as one accepts and lives the tension inherent in the paradox.

The philosophy of open marriage has little to offer those who see marriage as a genuine sharing of oneself and the central experiences of life. Relationships in many so-called modern marriages are more of convenience than of commitment. One's spouse is merely an instrument for personal pleasure and advancement.

The cross is a symbol of passage which signifies the leaving of the private world of the self, and the entry into the more expansive world of neighbor. The self is, so to speak, not left behind, but brought forward. The cross does not mean the destruction of the self, but rather, its enrichment through a joining with God and neighbor. This is why Jesus in his farewell address stated, "There is no greater love than this: to lay down one's life for one's friends" (Jn. 15:13). The gift of self in marriage is a restatement of Jesus' invitation to lay down one's life for another.

The presence of the cross can refer to an attitude of vulnerability and openness. It can also be attached to particular events when the giving takes place. Keeping in mind that spirituality and ministry in marriage concern basics, every area of life is open to the transforming power of the cross. From a conviction that the Lord's way is best, the married will not only accept those aspects of marriage which are "givens", for example, the particular temperaments and histories of each partner, but they will also look for opportunities to express generous concern and service. The transforming possibilities of the cross will be extended to include all the challenges of daily encounter where the creative tensions of marital life are played out.

A Dialogic Structure

Spirituality in marriage fosters the task of relational development in the pursuit of personal perfection. It emphasizes the communal spiritual life because this is the way the life journey of the married is shaped. All Christian spirituality is in some way based on relationships, on dialogue and *response*. It is never self-initiated because it is an answer to God's invitation to friendship, or to be more precise, toward an intimate love relationship. Self-made Christianity is a contradiction. But in marriage this response is structured particularly to including a response to God through one's spouse. Again, this is not intended as a move to reduce the importance or the integrity of the individual, but to point out that in marriage personal spiritual perfection is gained through loving exchange with one's spouse. Through this dynamic the spiritual journey of each is advanced.

This principle does not demand that all specifically spiritual acts be done in common. But it does imply that each will be open to seeing the other as participating in one's spiritual life and that, when helpful, common spiritual activity will be pursued. Shared prayer or other formal expressions of worship can be a source of great stimulation to the couple, or can also be a source of conflict within a marriage. From a general perspective, if two people share the more mundane aspects of life, they would deepen their common life by sharing prayer as well. But each partner may possess an individual spirituality, style of prayer life and worship which may be quite different from the other's. Respect and mutual sensitivity are important. Forced sharing may infringe upon religious freedom. All that can be given are principles for approaching this problem. Each couple is responsible for working this out in a way that respects both the individual journey to God and the common journey. This is no small problem given the number of mixed marriages where a couple may not share religious affiliation or, as sometimes happens, they share membership in a given church, but differ significantly in their style of participation.

Since the spiritual life potentially involves *everything* that is not specifically evil or sinful, the range of possible mutual cooperation is quite broad. While most may think that common prayer and common participation in the sacramental activity of the church are part of relational spirituality, other significant areas would include anything which enhances the love between the wife and the husband. A shared meal, a walk together in the neighborhood, even helping each other in common household projects qualify as elements of a vital marital spirituality.

The thought of Martin Buber is helpful in surfacing the importance of the I-Thou encounter as a structured experience through which the mystery of God is revealed. God is not only present in each person, but also between persons who love each other. This sacred space between lovers, like the space over the Ark of the Covenant in Solomon's temple, is a special locus of God's presence. And that divine presence is sensed even more as individuals actively seek to enrich that space with loving words and deeds.

The pattern of love giving birth to life, a central theme in the theology of marriage of Vatican II, also applies to the spiritual life of the married. The mutual love of wife and husband, expressed in the many ways appropriate to their relationships, is *the* essential ingredient of their spirituality. They are not obstacles for each other on the path to God, but rather aids in reaching the God who seems so distant, yet is immediately present in the space between them. Their love enriches their spiritual life.

The epistles of Paul mention how the presence of God in the temple takes on new meaning in Christianity. The primary place where God is to be found is in *people*, the new living temples of God. For the married, this presence is primarily in the marriage partner. This is part of the sacramental meaning of marriage. One's spouse becomes, however incredible this seems, a setting where God can be visited, encountered, and enjoyed.

The Style of Earthiness

The various qualities of marital spirituality and ministry which are being described here should not be viewed in isolation from each other, but are like the many faces of the same precious jewel. Each reflects a particular quality of conjugal spirituality. Those chosen for specific mention are those features which I believe are most overlooked in the transition from a spirituality for the single person to a spirituality more proper to the married. The earthy quality of marital spirituality, which is now emphasized, was perhaps the one feature most thought to be incompatible with spirituality in the early life of the church. It was believed by some that marriage was a less than perfect response to the Lord. Providing scriptural warrant for this position was a section in Paul's writings where he seems to side with those who denigrate the spiritual potential of marriage. Paul writes: "I should like you to be freed from worries. The unmarried man is busy with the Lord's affairs, concerned with pleasing the Lord; but the married man is busy with this world's demands and occupied with pleasing his wife. This means he is divided. The virgin — indeed, any unmarried woman — is concerned with things of the Lord, in pursuit of holiness in body and spirit. The married woman, on the other hand, has the cares of this world to absorb her and is concerned with pleasing her husband. I am going into this with you for your own good. I have no desires to place restrictions on you, but I do want to promote what is good, what will help you to devote yourself entirely to the Lord" (1 Cor. 7: 32-35).

I am not taking issue with the authority of Paul, but it is appropriate to call into question advice which he admitted was colored by a sense of the end of this world, which he felt was soon to occur. The primary issue seemed to be whether one's commitment to God was in some way lessened when one was also concerned about one's spouse. A literal reading of Paul leaves little doubt that he felt that such a division of allegiance arose in marriage with the result that the married were hindered from being entirely devoted to the Lord.

It must first be noted that the sayings of Jesus provide no support for this notion of divided loyalty. Jesus talked about the divided heart and the problem of serving two masters, but he never used marriage as an example of this problem. Nor did Jesus draw a hard line separating this world from the next. Actually he underscored a positive relationship between the two, pointing out often that the Kingdom has already begun in time with his coming. Nowhere does Jesus either directly or indirectly teach that there is any incompatibility between being married and full participation in the life of the Kingdom.

It appears, therefore, that Paul was driven to his position by a very limited, and no longer applicable, view of pending historical events. It should also be noted that Paul himself was very cautious about promoting his view by emphasizing that he was only offering a personal opinion, although he felt it was correct. His reasoning was as much practical (why enter marriage if the time left is so short?) as it was spiritual.

I focus on Paul's thought because it was picked up later by many Christian sects in support of their anti-world, anti-body, anti-sex viewpoints. Their writings unfortunately influenced Christian spirituality and it has only been in this century, with its appreciation of historical relativity, that Christians have felt free to deal critically with this somewhat heretical strain in the tradition. As a dangerous tendency, it has been labeled "angelism" in recent papal teaching.[7]

Corrective of this anti-creation spirituality is the sacramental approach offered here where *this world* — the world lovingly created by God — is the primary milieu for authentic religious response. In affirming and involving themselves in the redemptive process of transforming this world into a community of love and service, Christians continue the work begun by Jesus. For the married this process relates primarily to the worldly life of marriage itself. Other words of Paul, taken from the same letter which described the dividedness of the married, should, perhaps, be read as a balancing principle of spirituality: "You must know that your body is a temple of the Holy Spirit...So glorify God in your body" (1 Cor. 6: 19-20). Likewise, he might add, glorify God in the body of your spouse.

The Spirit of Fidelity

Marital fidelity is not adequately understood if it is only viewed as a test or a proof of one's marital promises. Rather, it is better to appreciate it as a quality of marital love which persists through the lifetime of the marriage. In this sense fidelity is a disposition in each marital partner in freely choosing the other, day after day, as the primary person with whom one walks on the journey of life. Fidelity frees one to journey, to run, even to race ahead with spontaneity, trust, and abandonment. It flourishes in the tension between the constancy of love, which creates security, and the risk of new love demanded by the changes in each person as time passes. To be faithful is to be flexible, always adjusting to new features in oneself and in one's spouse. This openness and sensitivity, already discussed as part of marital spirituality, provide fidelity with the personal information

---

[7]Paul VI, "Address to the Teams of Our Lady," 9.

required for fine-tuning the relationship in each period of significant change. Fidelity is directed both to the person involved and to their marital relationship. It is best thought of as relational fidelity.[8]

In a marriage, marked by fidelity, the marriage partner is chosen before all others. Yet this fidelity need not be taken as an infringement of personal freedom. Pure freedom is an illusion when one is considered most free when relieved of all interpersonal responsibility. This "no-strings-attached" approach hardly dignifies the notion of mature freedom. Entrance to freedom includes the act of decision which moves the person in a particular direction or toward a specific goal in life. The only real question worth pursuing is this: given the value and the requirement of decision-making, what is the best possible choice in a particular situation? Marital fidelity places one's marriage partner, along with the relationship itself, in the foreground of this discernment process.

Fidelity is nourished by each partner expanding and deepening marital love. It exists as an element of present love as it more effectively insures the future of the relationship. It is more than just holding on to past promises. Fidelity is conditioned by the many adjustments required in the marriage and by the communication, sexual and otherwise, which express the appreciation and satisfaction each finds in the other.

Fidelity is not a silent virtue, but active and responsive to the relational dynamics of daily life. It actively establishes the spouse as first in mind and heart. Infidelity can include not only sexual activity outside marriage, but it can also occur when a career, the quest for financial gain, personal hobbies or interests become more important than one's marriage. And this pattern of infidelity is often, although not always, one-sided. The breakdown of marital fidelity is commonly caused when both partners find other persons or activities "more interesting".

---

[8]See the thoughtful analysis of Andre Guindon, "Patterns of Sexual Fidelity and Ethical Paradigms," *Eglise e Theologie* 11 (1980), pp. 111 - 153.

Behind marital fidelity stands the fidelity of God which is a dynamic and vital aspect of God's love as well. Spiritual theology emphasizes God's closeness to humanity. God's relationship to each person is not like that of a person to an inanimate thing. It is interpersonal. Its mutuality is conditioned by the ebb and flow of change between the individuals involved. The biblical theme of "God with us" and "God for us" captures God as one who follows each person in steadfast love. Divine fidelity does not refer to a fixed position from which God rather staunchly views the affairs of humankind. God's fidelity is not static, but points to a feature of God's vitality. It responds to and holds precious every minute change in each person. God passionately cares for each person *in* the changes experienced as the journey of life unfolds.

The marital relationship is designed to embody or to replicate the same kind of loving concern. It is designed by God with a capacity for making real in a concrete relationship a feature of God's love. *This is the essence of Christian marital spirituality: actualizing in the marriage the faithful, enduring, and forgiving love life of God.* This is also the basis of its sacramental meaning. This also shows that one should not distinguish too sharply between spirituality and sacramentality. They are simply two ways of describing the same grace-enriched truth.

Marital spirituality clearly issues from the relation between wife and husband. There are also features of personal spirituality which flow from the uniqueness of each person before God. Marital spirituality adds to the personal, significant features of the relationship. It consciously and consistently affirms that the marriage itself is the well, the basic life-giving source of enriching one's life with God. The spirituality of the married is not apt to be as clear-cut or as organized as is a spirituality of a single person because it involves a combined response to both God and one's spouse. Marriage, of course, is not the only relationship which expresses the vitality of God's love in human form, but it does make this point with rigor and consistency.

Affirming the sacramental meaning of Christian marriage is the community's way of expressing this. The unique way marriage merits this sacramental meaning is discussed in the next chapter.

CHAPTER VIII: EXPERIENCED AS SACRAMENT

For more than a thousand years the official teaching of the church was practically silent in affirming the capacity of the married to experience God within the ordinary events of married life. Then, sensitized by theological developments, particularly by Aquinas, the church began to give greater attention to all created reality, marriage included, and its role in the divine drama of salvation. The axiom "grace builds on nature" provided the needed breakthrough enabling God's good creation to be appreciated in accord with the divine intention embedded in its foundation. Dead-end dualism, inherited from a pre-Christian, Hellenistic interpretation of creation or a "grace against nature" philosophy, was shown as inadequate for describing a world deeply loved by its Creator.

Unfortunately, that magnificent moment of theological enlightenment quickly waned as scholastic thought fell into misuse. The rich tapestry of Christian thought, woven by Aquinas and his contemporaries, was transformed by the hair-splitting categories of legalists. We recall the presence of voices in the church itself which called for a condemnation of Aquinas soon after his death. Perhaps, like other great thinkers, he was too advanced in his time to be appreciated and accepted into the mainstream of church thought. My purpose is not to remain within this historical framework, but simply to point out that the kind of sacramental theology presented here for Christian marriage has its roots both in a biblical substratum, and in a significant period of Catholic theological tradition.[1]

A Theology of Creation

Marriage is, in all its dimensions, an experience of creation. It is bodily; it is emotional; it is interpersonal. In relation to the traditional seven sacraments of the church, it is clearly the most earthy. Its qualifications for gaining identity as sacrament were historically dubious, given its close association with most things material. Its greatest liability was its sexual dimension. A church, in reading Paul's condemnation of the flesh as denouncing sex, needed little more to exclude sex and marriage from being listed among the good things created by God. Even the outcome of sexual relations, the child, was cast in an unfavorable light, being described as outside the boundaries of God's friendship until the cleansing waters of Baptism brought required purification from Original Sin. Theories explained this by referring to a sinful "contamination" communicated to the offspring by the ignominious way in which the child was conceived. Fortunately, most of this negative theology is found only in historical treatises; although it is worth remembering that if people could create distorted theology once, they can do it again.

Today's approach is based on an affirmation that the God of creation and the God of salvation are one. God created the universe with a purpose: That God's own goodness and

[1]For further reading on this see Peter Garland, *The Definition of Sacrament According to Saint Thomas*, Ottawa: University of Ottawa Press, 1959; Bernard Lonergon, *Grace and Freedom in Aquinas*, New York: Herder and Herder, 1971; and Edward Schillebeeckx, *Christ, The Sacrament of the Encounter with God*, New York: Sheed and Ward, 1963.

life was to be shared with others, particularly those created most like God, women and men. God warned in the commandments not to create images of God in stone, wood, or in sub-human animal form. God alone created adequate images capable of reflecting God's own goodness and love. And this was done right from the beginning. That first pair imprinted with God's image were named Adam and Eve.[2]

Some rather astounding ideas percolate through the biblical accounts of humanity's coming-to-be. Historians note that the culture responsible for creating the Adam and Eve story involved strong male dominance in marriage, family, and political life. That same culture viewed marriage as an institution whose primary role was insuring the continuation of the family or the tribe. Women's role in procreation and in the overall political life of the community was passive and compliant. Fascinating about the Adam and Eve story is that surprising emphasis is placed on their relationship to each other, with what might be termed the dehumanizing or alienating factors like dominance, shame, etc., coming only after the introduction of sin. The composer(s) of Genesis imagined for this couple a pristine, God-given capacity, a deep-seated possibility for a relationship uneffected by sin, yet compatible with created human nature. If there was a distortion of the image of God, blame wasn't to be laid at the feet of God, but placed before the couple because of their misdoing.

The account of creation in Genesis, while suggestive and indicative of many elements in contemporary experience (as all good and true stories have that capacity) cannot be presented as the last word. Creation "in the beginning" was only a beginning. The role and influence of Adam and Eve was to be surpassed in significance and effect by the one called by Paul, "the last Adam" (1 Cor 15:45). Jesus came to invest creation with new meaning and power; and, as in the case of marriage, to call the wife-husband relationship to a

---

[2] I refrain from discussing the issue relating to the historical identity of the first couple. I am more interested in affirming the symbolic meaning of our progenitors in light of the Genesis account of the beginning.

new level of accountability. Jesus announced that those exquisite possibilities of life, hinted at in descriptions of "the beginning" were now possible. While the fact of sin remained, its power to debilitate or even kill was taken away by Jesus, the Lamb of final offering.

In his wake a New Creation leaped to life filled with God's presence, power, and availability. Humanity remained free to exclude that presence and power from effecting personal and social life, but also at hand was the opportunity to exhaust the God-given, created potential of life. It remains a rightful boast of Roman Catholic thought that it did not accept the theory of defiled human nature where it was thought that no spark of the divine reality remained in creation after the Fall. No stand-off existed in Catholic theology between the powers of good and evil; the contest was tilted in favor of the good due to the Resurrection of the Lord and the presence of the Spirit in life. Creation may have been wounded by its contact with sin, but it was not destroyed. Traditionally Catholicism has maintained a sense of the sacramental, general appreciation of God's fidelity to creation. God is available at all moments when humanity is open to "touch" the God at hand.

Because of its sacramental emphasis, Catholicism is vulnerable to various forms of superstition and magic. This occurs when people either attempt to appropriate God's power by the use of material devices or they misunderstand the way God cooperates with human effort. God does not act in spite of us, or contrary to the ordinary dynamics of created potential. Rather, God "works" *within* human and created life. This is why Christianity speaks of the *vision* of faith, a Spirit-generated discernment, which allows the person to perceive within human life the real God.

It is possible to possess what might be called narrow-minded faith. Without good reason certain areas of life are excluded from the ambit of sacramental possibility. This seems to be what happened when marriage and its essential experiences were not identified as sacramental. Aspects of creation associated with strong human drive or emotion, plus those activities which humanity shared with lower animals, e.g. eating, drinking, and copulation, were determined as inconsistent with wholesome spirituality. Body and spirit were assumed to be opposed. Earth and heaven were separated by a chasm of infinite breadth.

Sacramental theology now teaches that sacramentality is not added atop creation like frosting on a cake, but rather, it is an inherent quality of creation itself. It comes from God's doing; we didn't put it there, but we do participate in its discovery. Good theological maps of the terrain of creation are valuable in this regard. The location of the treasure is not obvious. It is buried deep within. Past generations were misled by the anti-creation bias of Hellenistic thought. Today we may be deceived by a secular attitude which proclaims there is nothing "there" but the physical, the corporeal, and those illusive atoms and particles which constitute the cosmos.

Helpful in formulating a sacramental theology for today is a growing interest in the role which symbols play in human life. True symbols should not be thought of as mere signs which "stand for something else." Rather symbols embody that which is present deep within them. When a particular symbol involves both word and deed, it is capable of incorporating a richness of significance, a density of meaning which broadens our narrow or preconceived interpretation of life. The experience of rich symbol expands perceptions, feelings, and experiences in suggesting dimensions to reality beyond that which appears on the surface of things.[3]

Sacramental events in the church are more like symbols than signs because they invite the community to enter into the deep, divine realm of space and time. They invite contact with the always available, yet not always appreciated, presence and power of God. The quality of the sacramental event becomes quite important so that the full import of the symbol may be realized. This does not mean that by manipulation humanity can pull an absent God into the world, but

---

[3]On this point see Paul Ricoeur, *The Symbolism of Evil,* Boston: Beacon Press, 1967, p. 352.

rather people can be more readied to be drawn into God's space and time in sacramental events.

Human limitation prevents most people from maintaining a level of constant awareness of God's immediate presence, although the great mystics seem to have attained a modicum of that awareness. Most depend on certain moments or events which over the years have been identified as special occasions of God's availability. These have come to be known as the seven sacraments of the church. Whether more may be identified is not discussed here, although it is perfectly possible given the historical evidence that the church came to an awareness of its present sacramental understanding only gradually and who can say that a limit has been absolutely attained. Fortunately, Christian marriage has already earned this status, but it is always possible to find in it ever deeper meaning. Our quest for a more adequate theology of marriage is based on the growing appreciation of sacramental symbolism. Our starting point is a question as to what in Christian marriage expresses the presence and power of God.

Before responding to this question, one more idea deserves consideration. Along with a greater appreciation of the value of symbolic expression there is also a rediscovery of the church itself having sacramental meaning.[4] This establishes the importance of community as an ingredient of sacramentality. As ecclesial community, gathered in worship, prayer, and ministry, gains value and significance, so will the communal dimension of the sacraments, matrimony included, become more apparent. Relating to a sense of church and sacrament is the way contemporary Catholic theology incorporates in its analysis of sacrament an appreciation of the way God was present in the person of Jesus Christ. With the Word of God becoming flesh, a pattern of divine involvement is established which states that in the concrete person of the man from Nazareth, there is vitally present the Son of God, active and involved in the historical events recorded so vividly in the gospels. God lived in Jesus,

[4]See Vatican II, *Dogmatic Constitution of the Church*, 1-8.

and those who came in contact with this man saw, heard and touched God as God is present in created form. In this way, Jesus himself can be viewed as a sacrament.

With the resurrection and ascension of Jesus, the presence of God remained available because the Spirit of God dwelled within the community of disciples, the church. As the church itself gained life, God's presence and activity continued. Different from God's presence in Jesus, the created side of church life was effected by the limitations of sin and human frailty. Today this is referred to as the pilgrim status of the church. Its full perfection will occur only in the future. The refinement of its own life through continuous conversion, reflection, prayer, and good works are necessary for it to live up to its privileged calling as a sacrament of God's presence. While the phrase "ecclesial semper reformanda" (the church always in need of reform) was created as reaction to the Catholic Church by Protestant reformers, this approach is now accepted as a valid principle of life within the Catholic Church as is evidenced pointedly by the wholesale reforms inaugurated by Vatican II. Never allowed to be content or satisfied with its present status, the church is obliged to daily seek improvement of this for Christian marriage as well. With Christian married life being a distinct example of church life, it too is subsumed under the general mandate of seeking regular and sustained enrichment. Christian marriage can also be appreciated as the journey of pilgrims.

A Sacramentalization of God's Love

So why is Christian marriage a sacrament? Is it because it embodies a human love between wife and husband, a love so rich and splendid that it contains and expresses God's very own love. First captured in the prophetic literature of the Hebrew Scriptures, particularly in the book of Hosea, and later expressed in the letter to the Ephesians, marriage symbolizes God's faithful, focused, and intense love for humanity. John Paul II expresses this exquisitely in his apostolic exhortation on the family. "The communion of love between God and people, a fundamental part of the revelation and faith experience of Israel, finds a meaningful expression in the marriage covenant which is established between a man and a woman. For this reason the central word of revelation, 'God loves his people,' is likewise proclaimed through the living and concrete word whereby a man and a woman express their conjugal love. Their bond of love becomes the image and the symbol of the covenant which unites God and his people."[5]

Human relationships are initiated by a word of introduction, advanced by a word of promise, enriched by a word of commitment, and prolonged by a word of service. The focus on word as central to marriage is significant. This relates not only to an appreciation of the sexual expression as a special type of commitment language, but it also grasps the essential relational character of marriage. A person of quality is a person of his or her word. Word here implies more than simply a conveyor of information, although it commonly enough is reduced to that meaning. A good person's word is honest and sincere. One's word need not only be thought of as a vocal or written word. Human language is very broad and complex. Even deeds are a kind of word. What's most important however, is the word behind all one's words, whatever their form. Jesus was not described as expressing the words of God, but as God's fundamental word, God's basic utterance to humanity. In a like manner, papal teaching focuses on "the living and concrete word" expressing conjugal love.

This conjugal word of love is identified as the same word which declares that God loves his people. The conjugal word is therefore sacramental. It symbolizes and is empowered to express God's love. While not arguing that only marital love has this capacity, the Pope notes, nevertheless, that it is possible for this to happen in Christian marriage. Given the condition of the world and the church, he might also be suggesting that the word of love is greatly needed

[5]John Paul II, "On the Family," 12.

today. Where some may doubt or express cynicism that faithful, abiding, and honest love is possible, married Christians can give counter evidence that it is not only possible, it does happen.

Mentioned already was the passage in Ephesians calling attention to the connection between God's love and marriage. "For this reason, a man must leave his father and mother and be joined to his wife, and the two will become one body. This mystery has many implications; but I am saying it applies to Christ and the Church" (Eph 5:31-32 —Jerusalem Bible).

While no other passage in scripture is as important for the theology of marriage, it defies simple interpretation.[6] Some conclude that the main point is to underscore the relational quality existing between Christ and the church, and to offer his faithful and sacrificial love as a lesson for imitation by the married. Others see in the passage a reference to the experience of married love as a cipher or clue for understanding the nature of God's love as it is present in Jesus. The first approach argues that the "higher" relationship gives meaning to the "lower." The second focuses on the "lower" as pointing to the "higher." How one interprets the correspondence between the two covenantal bonds depends not so much on what is in the passage, but on the theological framework one brings to the text. Protestant theologians like Karl Barth underscore the "revelation" as coming from above. Catholic interpreters often reverse the direction of illumination so that its source is more from below. Still others, like Karl Rahner, will note that the comparison can operate in both directions. The divine covenant relationship provides clarity and completeness while the marital relation adds vitality and substance to the comparison.[7] The more one brings a genuine sacramental theology to the passage, the more the either/or option wanes as a sense of mutual

---

[6]A survey of interpretations is provided in J. P. Sampley *'And the Two Shall Become One Flesh': A Study of the Traditions in Ephesians 5:21-33,* Cambridge: Cambridge University Press, 1971.

[7]Karl Rahner, "Marriage as Sacrament," p.220.

illumination of marriage and the divine covenant occurs.

The divine covenant of Christ and the church is not identical with the marriage covenant. The former has God as one of the covenant partners. Unless one "divinizes"the marital union, and it should not be concluded that this has never been attempted, there cannot be an exact correspondence. The comparison between the two covenants is not a likening of the individuals involved, but rather a similarity in the type of relationship which exists between them.[8]

The common element is covenantal love: a love that is made founded by God's love in both cases. Marital love is *symbol* of God's love. When Christian marital love is real, honest, and genuine, it raises questions, awakens the imagination, and calls into question limited views of love's possibilities within the world. The sacrament of matrimony suggests that one who holds "unreasonable expectations" for the married need not be viewed as foolish or hopelessly naive.[9] This sacramental interpretation of marriage promotes an open-ended view of possibilities. Possibility is not reduced to fixed laws of human possibilities, but by human generosity and by God's creative Spirit which know no bounds. What is possible in marriage cannot be left to the statistics or findings of social scientists, however correct may be their perceptions or conclusions. In Christian marriage the effort of God is joined with that of the human spirit in creating a community of persons, a community of love.

A helpful way to describe the divine-human endeavor in marriage is to imagine God's creative love as a form of energy creating life, particularly communal life. Those familiar with the thought of Teilhard de Chardin will recognize a similar thought pattern in his theology. God is a limitless source of love-energy which empowers humanity in its relational life. All are created with a potential and a promise by God to be able to accomplish that which God

---

[8]Theories which use this passage as proof for male headship in marriage fail to appreciate this.

[9]See an application of this principle to all sacramental life by Regis Duffy, *Real Presence: Worship, Sacraments, and Commitment,* New York: Harper and Row, 1982.

intends. All human understanding of God's "desires" are themselves fragmentary although our knowledge is sufficient if we take the pains to discover what we ought to know. The maps possessed are adequate for finding the treasure. The attempt to grasp the truth of life is pursued against the background or horizon of mystery, the mystery which envelops life itself and God's relationship to us. As our knowledge and love deepen, so does our *participation* in that enveloping mystery expand. Progress through the stages of development may have all the paradoxical features which were presented in an earlier chapter on the seasons of marriage. Movements into seeming darkness may, in fact, be excursions into greater light. Our own self-generated illumination is often deceptive, as any recollection of the "clear" idea about life and people we had as teens will point out. The Socratic axiom that true wisdom is the knowledge of ignorance needs no further argument for the thinking adult.

The mystery of God, which generates and supports married life, can be dissected for analysis and understanding by pointing out the various levels of Christian marriage and how the presence of God's mystery relates to each. Christian marriage is as complex as any realm of life, and perhaps some of the inadequate descriptions of its life by theologians in the past can be traced to their discussion of only a single facet of its totality. For example, the debate between those who emphasize the covenantal side of marriage against theologies which stress its contractual elements need not result in an either/or dilemma. Both sides have a point to contribute, but they each describe different aspects of the relationship of sacramental meaning.

Before exploring levels of sacramental meaning, I would caution against a radical separation between them. They are "organically" related. In reality they each stand in mutual dependence. The energy of God permeates the whole as does the experience of Christian marriage itself. Five levels of Christian marriage appear as worthy of analysis and understanding. They are: 1) the Sexual, 2) the Creative, 3) the Loving, 4) the Ecclesial, and 5) the Spiritual. They move from that which is more physical to that which is more spiritual. There is no cause for removing the spiritual from the physical, but rather my claim that from the standpoint of this sacramental model, the spiritual *needs* the physical to become all that is possible, and *vice versa*!

SACRAMENTALIZED IN SEXUALITY

The first level of Christian marriage is the sexual. Being married, as woman *or* man, means that sexual differences, whatever their effect, are accepted and respected. The physical contact between the spouses is part of their sacramental experience. To include human sexual need does not necessarily demean the dignity of Matrimony. It is part of the raw material made sacred by being brought into the ambit of God's good creation.

The emphasis on the sexual is part of the historical tradition present in the Catholic approach to marriage. The official juridicial description of marriage established at the beginning of this century included specific reference to the physical. Church law described Christian marriage and the exchange it involved in the following way: "Marital consent is an act of the will by which each party gives and accepts a perpetual and exclusive right over the body (*'jus in corpus'*) for acts which are of themselves suitable for the generation of children. . ."[10] If one had only this text to create a Christian view of marriage, one's resources would be meager indeed. Taken alone, without reference to other features of their union, this approach manifests a rather narrow and incomplete appreciation of Christian marriage as sacramental. The definition was restated by Vatican II, thus amending the too narrow approach of an earlier period.

The sexual side of marriage includes more than physical or biological joining. Being woman or man influences much of that which designates our humanity. While it may be difficult to adequately specify a feminine or masculine

---

[10]Canon 1081, (Code of 1917). See also Theodore Mackin, *What is marriage*, pp. 192-224.

manner of orientation and response, it is nevertheless widely accepted that sexual distinctiveness is more than a matter of biology. Being woman or man cuts to the deepest experiences of being human. This broad appreciation of the sexual invites full valuing of the corporeal as it is drawn into the power and influence of God's energy which transforms this quite earthy aspect of marriage. Praised in the Song of Songs and given full attention and respect in Paul's writings in his invitation to glorify the Lord in our bodies, the sexual aspect of human life, although open to misuse or disregard, still participates in its own way in the building of the Kingdom of God.

As recognition of the spiritual value of marriage grows, a tendency may develop to denigrate the physical. Christian thought has had to fight its way clear of gnostic or spiritualist tendencies throughout its history and it cannot be assumed that this escape into the spiritual is no longer available. While God is pure spirit, we are not. Nor are we angelic. Our glory is rooted in our created natures, symbolically described in Genesis as coming from the humus of the earth. And in the same breath, it is noted that as woman and man, we are fashioned in the image of God — hardly a title of disrepute!

Positively, the inclusion of the sexual within the sacramentality of marriage alerts us to what John Paul II calls the nuptual meaning of the body.[11] Designed into creation itself is a reminder of our interpersonal nature. Without falling into a theory that woman and man are partial persons without each other, the Pope argues that in being created sexual, we find a kind of divine memorandum, a sign that we are not created as solitaries. We are social beings who are marked in our bodies with a clue about our deepest identity as created for God and for each other.

If the Word of God became flesh to reveal God's concern and love, is it not appropriate to search all examples of incarnated life to learn whether God might be revealing truth in other places as well? In Christian marriage this

[11]This is discussed in Joan Anzia and Mary Durkin, *Marital Intimacy*, pp. 1-14.

occurs when the sacramentality of marriage involves the acceptance and inclusion of the sexual within the sacred parameters of Matrimony.

Married Christians correctly express deep concern that their sexual relations be healthy and contribute positively to the deepening of their conjugal life. Whether the institutional church supports their solicitude in this area is not all that evident. In its general failure to develop a positive theology of sexuality, the church perhaps gives the impression that sex is not important for its married members, or that there is something about the sexual that impairs the purity of the Christian life. In earlier chapters some of the confusion and misdirection experienced in earlier theological endeavors were reviewed. Today the way appears clear to affirm the rightful, significant place of the sexual in God's good creation particularly in the life of the married.

SACRAMENTALIZED IN CREATIVITY

Closely associated to the sexual is a second level of sacramentality in Christian marriage, its capacity to be creative. While this aspect of marriage has already been explored in an earlier chapter, it is useful to apply its key aspects in the specific context of sacramentality.

It is no longer adequate to hold that the creative side of marriage is primarily defined by the biological union of the spouses. Vatican II insightfully noted that children were the result of the couple's conjugal *love*. This further points out why the levels of Matrimony, being described here, are not separated in life. Included in the creative feature of marriage is the "function" of caring for new life during pregnancy, birth, and during the vital formative years of the child. To be responsible in the decision to procreate entails a realistic assessment of one's ability to meet the challenges of "creating" during this entire impressionable period.

Anthropologists describe the origin of marriage and the family largely in terms of the child's need for on-going protection, nourishment, and education into the complexities of culture and society. As societal institutions, marriage and the family owe their inception to the manifold needs of the child. While the manner in which a given marital and family unit accomplishes this task will vary historically and cross-culturally, it remains as a fundamental task even today.

Including creativity within the sacrament of Matrimony emphasizes the out-going or expansive nature of Christian marriage. Marriage can be lived as an institution of isolation, where the couple extract or excuse themselves from wider society to form a life of closed-togetherness. This orientation contradicts the Christian life as involving ever wider and wider realms of care and concern. A characteristic of genuine human and Christian love is the way it involves one deeper and deeper in God's creation. This is destroyed when marriage turns in upon itself. It is worth asking whether this inwardness is nothing more than a form of narcissism or radical self-centeredness. When fulfilling one's own desires becomes the whole basis for living, it turns the dynamics of the marital relationship into a self-serving mode where each partner simply uses the other for personal gain.

Given the traditional emphasis on marital procreation and education, it is worth asking why there is no specific sacrament of Christian parenting. It would seem that nurturing, an essential feature of parenting, symbolizes the creative and nurturing love of God. The absence of a special sacrament for parenting is due, I believe, to the relation of parenting to marriage. While this should not be taken as a critique in any way of single parents, whose task is certainly quite difficult, nevertheless, it is necessary to hold that the ordinary pattern of parenting is appropriately done in the setting of marriage. Just as the vowed religious life needs no further sacrament to specify its meaning and sacredness because of its relation to Baptism, so the same can be said for parenting.

Integrating the tasks of parenting with the demands of marriage is no small endeavor. Numerous studies have shown a decrease in marital happiness upon the arrival of the first child. This should not be surprising if one analyses the time, effort, and involvement required in the care of infants. Yet, children should not be used as an excuse for exempting oneself from the requirement of sustaining the marital relationship. Balancing marital and parental responsibilities requires good judgment in allocating time and energy. This is obvious. But there is another issue which concerns the inclusion and integration of both spouse and children on the affective level. The love of spouse and the love of children need not be experienced as competitive. Hopefully marital love can grow to include parental love. As a practical matter, this is difficult where the care of children is judged the responsibility of just one partner. A key to the integrative process is when both wife and husband care for the children as expressions of love for each other. The value of both parents' involvement in the daily care of children is gaining in popularity. This trend benefits both the child and the marriage. With these advantages, it is a wonder that its acceptance is so recent.

SACRAMENTALIZED IN LOVING

Within the five identified levels of sacramentality, a central position is occupied by Christian marital love. Like the love of God which it mirrors, this love illumines and affects all the other levels. In harmony with the insight of Paul in chapter thirteen of First Corinthians, without love in marriage there will be nothing of real significance. The sexual attraction between woman and man, and their creative abilities in marriage gain sacramental significance from the love between the wife and husband. It is that special elective, comprehensive, and unconditional love between them which makes real in the world God's love of the same genre.

Christian marital love is human, heterosexual love for a specific person. It retains human form all the while it takes on the further meaning of sacramentality. It follows the many laws of human change and growth. As was described in the chapter on the seasons of marital life, it normally undergoes a sequence of changes which either enhance or deplete its vigor. The value of Matrimony flows from its being so human. Just as real water and real bread are needed for the sacraments of Baptism and Eucharist, genuine human, heterosexual love is necessary for Matrimony. It is the "intimate partnership of married life and love" which God has authored into creation as a sacramental expression of God's own love.[12]

The church, in moving its emphasis in marriage from a more juridicial description of a ratified and consummated union to a focus on marital love, has strained its ability to make clear and unencumbered decisions as to either the presence or absence of the Sacrament of Matrimony in a given couple. Since Vatican II's effort to base an ecclesial description of Christian marriage on more biblical and personalistic categories, the tribunals of the church have altered their categories for determining the existence of Matrimony in particular cases. The process of creating ever more adequate criteria is still occurring and will probably continue in this vein for the foreseeable future.[13]

Love is as complex as any human phenomenon and there is no lack of experts or quasi-experts attempting to define, redefine, and undefine love. A certain wisdom exists in the argument of those who contend that love does not belong in a system of evaluation which is given the task of deciding either its presence or absence. Sometimes not even those in a given marriage know for sure!

Yet every form of Christian life, whether it be of the married or the single, cannot escape the invitation and the task to love as it applies in each particular state of life. Its ambiguity, its mysterious character, its oblique yet inescapable association with human emotions, and not the least, its cost to those who would follow its full demands, cannot rule out its central role in Christian marriage. In focusing upon love as central, we have not so much found a solution to its proper definition, rather we have uncovered a multitude of

[12]Vatican II, *Pastoral Constitution on the Church in the Modern World*, 48.

[13]For a comprehensive presentation of this see Theodore Mackin *What is Marriage*, pp. 283-327. See also *Divorce Ministry and the Marriage Tribunal*, edited by James Young, Ramsey: Paulist Press, 1982.

questions which defy easy answers, or much more, a facile response in practice. No wonder so few of the contemporaries of Jesus really understood the man. Today our struggle to define the Sacrament of Matrimony in the neat categories of the past may indicate we are closer to the truth, which is rooted in mystery, and further from human categories which are more apt to enslave than to free.[14]

SACRAMENTALIZED
AS REFLECTING SALVATION

The fourth level of marriage involving the Sacrament of Matrimony denotes the association of the conjugal covenant with the covenant between Christ and his church. First it should be noted that the correspondence between the Christ-church relationship and marriage is not the only relation which symbolizes God's salvific love. All loving interpersonal relationships are capable of symbolizing Christ's love. The dedicated love of countless single lay people, vowed religious, and priests all participate in that incredible love between Christ and the church. Paul's letters are filled with invitations to love as Christ did, and to respond to the invitation of Christ's love in full obedience and service. In fact, the main point of the already-quoted Ephesians text may be that *even* marriage can be brought into the ambit of Spirit-empowered relationships! In the cultural setting of that affirmation, it may have been quite surprising to make this declaration. And this should not be surprising if we recall the difficulty within the church of admitting marriage into its listing of sacraments. If it was not obvious to those who formulated Christian theology for more than a thousand years, why should it have been clear to the first-century Christians in Ephesus who were recipients of those inspired words?

While all Christian relationships draw life and meaning from the relationship between Christ and the church, marriage is so structured that it embodies certain marks or

---

[14]An excellent account of this is given in Bernard Haring, *Free and Faithful in Christ*, Vol. 2, pp. 433-438.

features of that foundational covenant. The tradition of the church has long valued these characteristics. They are essential to Matrimony as a sacrament. Christian marriage involves the attributes of exclusivity and indissolubility. Rephrased in a more contemporary way, the marital relationship includes a focus and fidelity unlike any other human association. Each partner centers attention and love on the other and sustains it by intention and fact until death does them part.

Exclusivity, focus, or centering are ways of decribing the choice of another, a sexual opposite, for creating a relationship and a sharing of life involving all the significant projects associated with their common life. Marriage is an act of discrimination where the marriage partner gains a privileged status ahead of all others. How exclusivity is lived out in the concrete depends on many factors inherent within each particular marriage. Part of the risk involved in exclusivity is an openness to learn about and accept aspects of the spouse as yet unknown. Like the risk involved in the act of faith, this trust in an unknown may seem foolhardy to those who must control reality before entering its arena. Christians, on the other hand, move ahead convinced that reality is trustworthy.[15]

This quality of marriage corresponds to that feature of God's love where God elects and loves each concrete person intensely, unconditionally, and constantly, with a passion and depth humans can only roughly emulate. Yet in Christian marriage an echoing of this quality of God's love is attempted. Using echo as an image of this dynamic is particularly apropos because an echo is totally dependent on an originating sound. The echo provides evidence of its source, but it cannot perfectly replicate it. For the echo to occur, conditions must be right for the reverberations to be repeated. The source of the sound waves projects them against a hard object, which, in turn, reflects that same sound so that the hearer will experience the passage of the sound at least twice. The nature of the reflecting body

[15]See Karl Rahner "Marriage as Sacrament," p. 208.

determines the quality of the echo. The larger its surface, the better its echoing ability will be. The volume and quality of the echo is also affected by the distance the sound wave has to travel before it is reflected.

Applied to marriage the ability to reflect God's elective love is increased in proportion to the love present between wife and husband. The larger their love, the more God's love will be present in their love. Also, the closer the couple is to God, the more efficacious wll be their capacity to echo divine, passionate love.

Indissolubility, fidelity, and sustenance echo God's faithful and forgiving love for each person and for God's people. God's ways of merciful forgiveness are to be embodied in all human relationships, but it has a particular force in marriage. In not parting — a minimal requirement for echoing God's fidelity — the couple reflects the staying power of God's love. This task is not done alone as God joins with the couple promising all needed assistance to keep them together.

Each partner in Christian marriage is invited to exemplify God's faithful and forgiving love. But as divorce statistics tragically indicate, many apparently well-intentioned couples fail to complete their marital journey. Some appear more or less doomed from the start. They simply lack an adequate capacity for creating the quality of love relationship necessary for Christian marriage. Their inadequacies may be physical, psychological, or circumstantial. Their stories are often heard by church tribunals and in the privacy of the Sacrament of Reconciliation. Mercifully and rightfully, their attempted marriages are declared to have never reached the status of Christian marriage. Those so judged are free to marry in the church and any children born from the original union are viewed as legitimate according to the law of the church.

Each divorce has a history which usually contains elements of human weakness, finitude, and limitation (which moralists term "ontic evil"). But also present in many situations is sin, self-centeredness, and pride (moral evil). Widespread societal acceptance of divorce as a solution to marital difficulty has made it easier for many to view divorce as an option where before it would not even have been brought to mind. Higher expectations of marital happiness also create a climate where many become dissatisfied and chose to divorce rather than remain in a less than desirable marriage.

Most biblical scholars interpret Jesus' prohibition of divorce as absolute. The early church, however, probably modified his view even before the final words of the New Testament were written down.[16] Jesus based his response on a reference to the original intent of God as the basic structures of creation were established. Jesus called the married to a vsion of their life which corresponded to that founding situation. Nothing is recorded concerning how Jesus felt about those who were unable to reach that ideal. Certainly his own pastoral approach to the divorced, as exemplified in the story of the woman at the well, shows clearly forgiveness and sensitivity to ongoing need for spiritual wellbeing in the divorced.

Divorce is an issue of continuing concern for the church. John Paul II has offered hope to the divorced by affirming their membership in the church as they continue "the works of charity" which can hardly be done by one who would be thought of as living in a state of sin.[17] Divorce fractures the symbolism relating to the fidelity inherent in the Christ-church relationship. The experience of divorce itself is tragic, as those Christians who have been through it will be the first to testify. For those who do fail, the church now expresses deep pastoral concern, or as the Pope states, "The church will therefore make untiring efforts to put at their disposal her means of salvation."[18]

While there is little indication that the Catholic Church is about to change its present discipline regarding divorce and

---

[16]For a recent interpretation of the relevant passages which refer to divorce, see George W. MacRae, "New Testament Perspectives on Marriage and Divorce," in *Ministering to the Divorced Catholic*, edited by James J. Young, New York: Paulist Press, 1979, pp. 37-50.

[17]John Paul II, "On the Family," 84.

[18]*Ibid.*

remarriage, there is sufficient reason to at least discuss some possibilities which may more effectively bring the divorced and remarried into greater participation in fullness of ecclesial life. It cannot be argued that those in second marriages have committed an unforgivable sin.

While an increasingly large number of divorced and remarried Catholics cannot be the sole reason for a rethinking of this matter in the church, it should be added that some of the theological foundation for past church discipline is worth reconsideration. About eight hundred years ago the church stressed that the bond (*vinculum*) created in Christian marriage existed almost apart from the couple. Once it was established it could not be severed. Warrant for this approach was found in Scripture: What God had established, no one could sunder. This approach was formulated at a time when theology described two levels of reality where significant events occurred. One was natural and physical; the other was supernatural and spiritual. Humanity, graced by God, inhabited both realms. Certain human acts created effects in the supernatural realm. In many cases, particularly as a result of participation in the sacraments, effects became permanent. Baptism, Confirmation, and Orders caused a lasting change in the one receiving those sacraments. The result of Matrimony was the bond which existed until the physical death of one of the spouses. The "bond theory" of Matrimony described the sacrament as initiated by the exchange of marriage vows and confirmed by the first event of sexual intercourse.

Recent Catholic theology has focused on the interpersonal love relationship as essential to the sacrament. This love is *between* the wife and husband; it does not exist apart from them or, to use the construct of an earlier era, above them in some kind of metaphysical form. Today the question might be this: If marital love expires, does Christian marriage continue to exist? At the present time opinion is divided. Given the difficulty of defining the kind of love necessary for Christian marriage to be sacramental, particularly in a manner that would be useful for its use in church tribunals, some church officials remain skeptical about using human love as a sacramental necessity.[19] It is asked whether or not marital love extinguished can become re-ignited. Is it not central to Christian belief that life is more powerful than death? Forgiveness can replace hurt. Amendment can bind broken relationships. Forceful arguments can be marshalled to support hesitancy in changing the present discipline even when marital love seems to have passed away.

Yet, it is also apparent that many couples find their marriage filled with nothing but indifference or even hatred. They may be so distanced from each other that no reasonable possibility suggests that their love for each other will ever exist again. Prolonged and serious attempts to reconcile or to find the lost pieces of their marriage are often tried before the divorce decree is signed. Experience today indicates that most couples divorce out of desperation as a painful conclusion when no other option is available. The testimony that "it just didn't work out" is given regretfully. The pain of those passing through this is understood in the church which now offers in most areas supportive ministry to divorced Catholics.

Life must go on. Some divorced persons choose the single state. Their witness in fidelity to the church's present teaching concerning the lasting effect of one's marriage is often heroic. But what of those who, for many positive reasons, decide to enter a second marriage? It is assumed here that, at least according to the present church law, their first marriage cannot be annulled. From most indications, it was a Christian marriage. It simply ended, at least for its participants.

First, the intent of Jesus should be retained. Christian marriage is designed by God as a lifelong union. To argue that this goal is impossible or unreasonable is to doubt God's promise to provide what is needed to reach that goal. Marital failure cannot be blamed on God. In some instances it cannot be blamed on both parties of the marriage, either. While the reasons for failure often point to both spouses, it

[19]See Theodore Mackin, *What is* Marriage?, pp. 283-350.

can happen that the breakdown is caused by only one party. Divorce, in other words, does not necessarily imply moral failure.

Christianity has consistently stood for the possibility of evil. Convinced, however, that the Lord forgives, the church has reached out to the sinner with the hope that this forgiveness would be accepted in sorrow and out of an intent to sin no more. Christians are familiar with this dynamic.

Should this not be available to the divorced and remarried? Recall that papal teaching has moved beyond the taditional "state of sin" condition of these people by affirming their capacity for good works, prayer, and involvement in the life of the Christian community.[20] To sustain one's journey with the Lord rightfully invites the support of the church. Does this imply that the church is disregarding the fact of divorce and remarriage? Not at all, but it applies power of forgiveness which has the effect of restoring the individuals to church life.

Suppose that according to either church tribunal or the individuals involved, the first marriage was sacramental? If a second marriage is attempted, can it have the same ecclesial status as the first? Throughout its history, the Orthodox Church has allowed for these second marriages, but they are not given sacramental standing. A special ritual is used for their enactment which is more like a rite of reconciliation. A central feature of authentic sacramental marriage is its symbolic power to disclose God's fidelity. That feature is missing in these second marriages. If the sacrament is a source of divine revelation, a means which God uses to communicate to humanity, the symbol itself must be as clear as possible.

Supporting this approach is a pastoral value which holds that the salvation and sanctification of people is foremost. This principle stands behind the longstanding practice of the Orthodox Church and other non-Catholic Christian churches. Paul himself had this in mind when dealing with the issue of divorce in the young Christian community at Corinth in writing, "God has called you to live in peace" (1

---

[20]John Paul II, *On the Family*, 84.

Cor. 7:15). As the church attempts to bring life to its members, it will do so in a way that balances the invitation to full discipleship with a realism admitting to failure and sin. Of critical importance in marriage is its capacity to embody within that relationship God's faithful love. While contemporary pressures exist which make the ideal even more a challenge, these constraints cannot be used as an excuse for lowering the ideal. The divorced themselves often resist any compromise of the ideal they sought to attain. The church as a whole, like each of its members, is a pilgrim on the way to God. While a desire for perfect answers or solutions is appropriate, just as real is the impossibility of achieving that goal. This is part of "the untiring efforts" of the church mentioned above by the pope in his attempt to provide a pastoral response in this difficult situation.[21]

Christian marriage presents values to the church and the wider society which are without question. The bond within Christian marriage is, above all, an interpersonal union.[22]It establishes as "we" without destroying the integrity or uniqueness of the covenanting partners. Within that relationship are qualities which echo paramount features of the relationship between Christ and the church particularly in their faithful attachment which has life-creating possibilities. Christ has joined with the church for the sake of spiritual fertility. It is a relationship bent on bringing abundant life to all who would place themselves within its saving power. This also indicates that a counter-symbol is created when the couple turns inward and thereby renders impotent the power of Christian marriage to augment life for others. The symbolism is rendered meaningless in marital separation and divorce. The spirituality of marriage, as was indicated in an earlier chapter, must have this generative

---

[21]For a sensitive and balanced discussion of the divorce/remarriage issue, see Gerald S. Twomey, *When Catholics Marry Again: A Guide for the Divorced, Their Families, and Those Who Minister To Them*, Minneapolis: Winston Press, 1982.

[22]This is discussed in a work written in 1960 by John Paul II before his election to the pontificate. See Karol Wojtyla, *Love and Responsibility*, New York: Farrar, Straus, Gerouix, 1981, pp. 84-88.

ministerial force, or it will fail in expressing God's creative love into the future.[23]

SACRAMENTALIZING GOD'S OWN LIFE

The deepest level of mystery touched by Christian marriage is in the way it is invited and empowered to live God's own life. This momentous idea is captured in the simple phrase, "Matrimony is a graced relationship." The theology of grace is a rich resource for Christian reflection, yet because it is often explained in almost physical categories, and not in relational terms, it fails to exercise much influence on the religious imagination. It is also thought of by many as a static gift which makes it seem more like something one has or possesses. Too narrowly the sacraments of the church are approached as rituals through which God's grace is distributed. The use of that type of language makes it difficult to think of grace as anything other than something one receives for being good.

A more enlightened reading of Scripture and theology has brought the church to expand its understanding of grace as, first of all, God's gift of friendship, and second, as an empowering gift to live God's own life. We are invited to live in God as God lives in us. We do not lose our identity in this union, but, in fact, become more like that person God imagined when we were first created, and, therefore, reach personal maturity. Because the gift of that new life is from God, we cannot earn or merit this privileged status. It is offered to us as God's surprising gift to us. Reception and celebration of this gift occurs in the Sacrament of Baptism. Continued affirmation of its presence, that is of our continuing life in God, takes place in the Eucharistic celebration. What occurs in Matrimony is a refining of the Baptismal commitment in and through one's marital partner.

God's own life is relational. Belief in God as Trinity expresses the conviction that God is not a solitary, but lives in community. The intense love present in God is between

[23]See more about this in David Thomas, *When God is at Home in Your Family*, St. Meinrad: Abbey Press, 1978, pp. 51-69.

individuals or persons. Here our language stretches, of course, because we are only able to use created images and words to speak of God. Relationality itself gives definition to the various members of God. The Father (or Parent as some would have it to avoid attributing sexuality to God) is defined by there being Son (or Generated One). The Spirit is because of the loving ferment between the Others. A totally accurate map of God's own trinitarian life will have to wait for a later date and "location." Yet within Christian circles it is acknowledged that God's own life is communitarian and loving, and creation itself exists because of God's free desire to extend divine life to others.

In married love, therefore, is found a deeper love which stands as both origin and final goal of conjugal love. And like God's love, marital love is creative. Married Christians can truly be identified as cooperators with God in the creation of new life on the level of biological causality and even more deeply on the level of spiritual generativity.

This sense of sacramentality arises from its deepest roots. The couple, first drawn into the mystery of God's life at Baptism, plunge more deeply into that same mystery as they enter into each other's lives. The process is dynamic and gradual because it follows the ordinary tempo of relational life. The experiential dimensions of this have hardly been explored in formal Christian thought. There are moments of greater or more intense awareness, e.g., the wedding liturgy, the birth of the first child, the making-up after the first fight, or that special time when everything seems to come together. These will be somewhat different for each couple. As an experience and as symbol of God's creative love, Matrimony will always be somewhat opaque, and somewhat bathed in brightness. Like ecclesial life in general, it possesses its own pilgrim status which makes living within its boundaries and reflecting upon its meaning always open to more experience, understanding, and communication.

Perhaps this is partly why Jesus, when it came time for him to unveil the beginning in the signs which indicated that the Kingdom had begun, chose a wedding feast. For symbolized in marriage is that which all are called to create — a life that is one with God and one with each other. Jesus may not have formally instituted the Sacrament of Matrimony at Cana, but he felt comfortable in contributing to the continuation of the feast and accepting this all so human relationship as a special indicator that differences can be overcome and faithful love is possible. Christian marriage is, therefore, a genuine sign/symbol/sacrament that God's presence, love, and power are present in the real world, and that the married can, if willing, make God quite real in bed, board, babies, and backyard. And if it took the church so long to come to this awareness, it may be due to its failure to discuss the married with Christians who were married. They seemed to have had a sense of it right from the beginning.

For Further Reading

Chapter I

Dominian, Jack. *Marriage, Faith and Love.* New York: Crossroad Publishing Co., 1982.

Duhl, Bunny S. *From the Inside Out and Other Metaphors: Creative and Integrative Approaches to Training in Systems Thinking.* New York: Brunner/Mazel, Publishers, 1983.

Fowler, James W. *Becoming Adult, Becoming Christian.* New York: Harper & Row, 1984.

Haughton, Rosemary. *The Passionate God.* New York: Paulist Press, 1981.

John Paul II. *On The Family.* Washington, DC: U.S. Catholic Conference, 1982.

Kasper, Walter. *Theology of Christian Marriage.* New York: Seabury Press, 1980.

Lane, Dermot A. *Foundations for a Social Theology.* New York/Ramsey: Paulist Press, 1984.

Shea, John. *Stories of God.* Chicago: Thomas More Press, 1978.

Tracy, David. *Blessed Rage For Order.* New York: Seabury Press, 1975.

Whitehead, Evelyn and Whitehead, James. *Marrying Well.* Garden City: Doubleday, 1981.

Chapter II

Buber, Martin. *I and Thou.* New York: Charles Scribner's Sons, 1970.

Ford, Edward. *Choosing to Love: A New Way to Respond.* Minneapolis: Winston Press, 1983.

Ford, Edward and Englund, Steven. *Permanent Love.* Minneapolis: Winston, 1979.

Mace, David. *Love and Anger in Marriage.* Grand Rapids: Zondervan, 1982.

May, Rollo. *Love and Will.* New York: W. W. Norton, 1969.

Perkins, Pheme. *Love Commands in the New Testament.* New York: Paulist Press, 1982.

Pittenger, Norman. *Unbound Love.* New York: Seabury Press, 1976.

Rahner, Karl. *The Love of Jesus and the Love of Neighbor.* New York: Crossroad, 1983.

Shea, John. *An Experience Named Spirit.* Chicago: Thomas More Press, 1983.

Sternberg, Patricia. *Be My Friend: The Art of Good Relationships.* Philadelphia: Westminster Press, 1983.

Chapter III

Barnhouse, Ruth and Holmes, Urban (eds.). *Male and Female.* New York: Seabury Press, 1976.

Blenkinsopp, John. *Sexuality and the Christian Tradition.* Dayton: Pflaum, 1969.

Davis, Charles. *Body as Spirit.* New York: Seabury Press, 1976.

Donnelly, Dody. *Radical Love: An Approach to Sexual Spirituality.* Minneapolis: Winston Press, 1984.

Gallagher, Charles A., *et al. Embodied in Love: Sacramental Spirituality and Sexual Intimacy.* New York: Crossroad Publishing Co., 1983.

Hanigan, James P. *What Are They Saying About Sexual Morality.* New York/Ramsey: Paulist Press, 1982.

Keane, Philip. *Sexual Morality.* New York: Paulist Press, 1977.

Kilgore, James E. *The Intimate Man: Intimacy and Masculinity in the 80's.* Nashville: Abingdon Press, 1984.

Nelson, James B. *Between Two Gardens: Reflections on Sexuality and Religious Experience.* New York: The Pilgrim Press, 1983.

Sapp, Stephen. *Sexuality, the Bible and Science.* Philadelphia: Fortress Press, 1977.

Silbermann, Eileen Zieget. *The Savage Sacrament*. Mystic, CT: Twenty-third Publications, 1983 (subtitled: *A Theology of Marriage After American Feminism*).

Thomas, David (ed.). *Christian Reflection on Human Sexuality*. St. Meinrad: Abbey Press, 1978.

Chapter IV

Lederer, Wm., and Jackson, Don. *The Mirages of Marriage*. New York: W. W. Norton, 1968.

Mackin, Theodore. *What is Marriage?* New York: Paulist Press, 1982.

Peters, William. *What Your Wedding Can Be*. St. Meinrad: Abbey Press, 1980.

Schillebeeckx, Edward. *Marriage: Secular Reality and Saving Mystery*. New York: Sheed & Ward, 1965.

Chapter V

Bach, George and Wyden, Peter. *The Intimate Enemy*. New York: Avon, 1968.

Brenneman, Helen. *Marriage: Agony and Ecstasy*. Scottdale: Harold Press, 1975.

Clinebell, Howard. *Growth Counselling for Marriage Enrichment*. Philadelphia: Fortress Press, 1975.

Greeley, Andrew M. *The Young Catholic Family*. Chicago: Thomas More Press, 1980.

Hart, Kathleen Fischer and Hart, Thomas N. *The First Two Years of Marriage*. New York/Ramsey: Paulist Press, 1983.

Lee, Robert and Casebier, Marjorie. *The Spouse Gap*. Nashville: Abingdon, 1971.

Littauer, Florence. *After Every Wedding Comes a Marriage*. Eugene: Harvest House Publishers, 1981.

Mace, David and Mace, Vera. *We Can Have Better Marriages*. Nashville: Abingdon, 1974.

Miller, Sherod *et al. Straight Talk: A New Way to Get Closer to Others by Saying What You Really Mean.* New York: Rawson, Wade Publishers, Inc., 1981.

Wright, H. Norman. *Seasons of a Marriage.* Ventura: Regal Books, 1982.

Chapter VI

Curran, Dolores. *Traits of the Healthy Family.* Minneapolis: Winston, 1983.

Haring, Bernard. *Free and Faithful in Christ. Vol. 2.* New York: Seabury Press, 1979.

Kenny, James and Kenny, Mary. *Whole Life Parenting.* New York: Continuum, 1982.

Larson, Jim. *Rights, Wrongs and In-Betweens: Guiding Our Children to Christian Maturity.* Minneapolis: Augsburg Press, 1984.

Lief, Nina R. with Mary Ellen Fahs. *The First Year of Life: A Guide for Parenting.* New York: Sadlier, 1982.

McGinnis, James and McGinnis, Kathleen. *Parenting for Peace and Justice.* Maryknoll: Orbis Books, 1982.

Olson, David H. *Families, What Makes Them Work.* Beverly Hills: Sage Publications, 1983.

Satir, Virginia. *Peoplemaking.* Palo Alto: Science and Behavior Books, 1972.

Westerhoff, John. *Bringing Up Children in the Christian Faith.* Minneapolis: Winston, 1980.

Chapter VII

Hays, Edward. *Secular Sanctity.* New York: Paulist Press, 1980.

Leckey, Dolores. *The Ordinary Way.* New York: Crossroad Publishing Co., 1982.

Mouw, Richard. *Called to Holy Worldliness.* Philadelphia: Fortress Press, 1980.

Nouwen, Henri. *With Open Hands.* Notre Dame: Ave Maria Press, 1972.

Thomas, David (ed.). *Marital Spirituality*. St. Meinrad: Abbey Press, 1978.

Thomas, David. *When God Is at Home with Your Family*. St. Meinrad: Abbey Press, 1978.

Whitehead, Evelyn and Whitehead, James. *Christian Life Patterns*. Garden City: Doubleday, 1979.

_____. *Seasons of Strength: New Visions of Adult Christian Maturing*. Garden City: Doubleday, 1984.

Chapter VIII

Cooke, Bernard. *Sacraments and Sacramentality*. Mystic, CT: Twenty-third Publications, 1983.

Guzie, Tad. *The Book of Sacramental Basics*. New York: Paulist Press, 1982.

Ho, Man Keung. *Building a Successful Intermarriage Between Religions, Social Classes, Ethnic Groups or Races*. St. Meinrad: Abbey Press, 1984.

Mackin, Theodore. *Divorce and Remarriage*. New York/Ramsey, Paulist Press, 1984.

Martos, Joseph. *Doors to the Sacred*. Garden City: Doubleday, 1981.

Rahner, Karl. "Marriage as Sacrament" in *Theological Investigations*, Vol. 10. New York: Seabury Press, 1974.

Twomey, Gerald. *When Catholics Marry Again*. Minneapolis: Winston, 1982.

Young, James (ed.). *Ministering to the Divorced Catholic*. New York: Paulist Press, 1979.

Young, James. *Divorcing, Believing, Belonging*. New York/Ramsey, Paulist Press, 1984.